EXAMINING THE EVIDENCE
Nineteenth-century England

Editors: Leonard W. Cowie *and* Evelyn E. Cowie

Education

EXAMINING THE EVIDENCE
Nineteenth-century England

Editors: Leonard W. Cowie *and* Evelyn E. Cowie

Education

Evelyn E. Cowie

METHUEN EDUCATIONAL LTD
London · Toronto · Sydney · Wellington

First published 1973 by Methuen Educational Ltd
11 New Fetter Lane, London EC4P 4EE

Filmset in Photon Times 11 on 13 pt. by
Richard Clay (The Chaucer Press) Ltd, Bungay, Suffolk
and printed in Great Britain by
Fletcher & Son Ltd, Norwich

SBN 0 423 44870 6 HB
423 44880 3 PB

Contents

Acknowledgements

Permission to reproduce illustrations is gratefully acknowledged to Northampton Public Library for page 13; the University of Durham Library for page 54; Saint David's College, Lampeter, for page 61; the Curators of the Bodleian Library for page 66; the University of London School, Greater London Council Print Collection, for page 77; the Victoria and Albert Museum for page 101; the Greater London Council Members' Library for page 137.

1 The opening of a new era

Sir William Blackstone in his book, *Commentaries on the Laws of England*, reminded his readers that 'a parent conferred no considerable benefit on his child by bringing him into the world, if he afterwards entirely neglected his culture and education and suffered him to grow up like a mere beast to lead a life useless to others and shameful to himself'. Writing at the end of the eighteenth century, he maintained that the enlightenment of the masses was vital to safeguard freedom and democracy. To achieve this he advocated compulsory schooling.

The first report of the Society for Bettering the Condition of the Poor, published in 1809, shows that those who sympathized with Blackstone had found it difficult to justify their views during the French Revolution:

> I am aware that there have been many and still are some pious and conscientious Christians who dread the consequences of a general diffusion even of elementary knowledge among the poor. The miseries which have attended the very name of equality in a neighbouring Kingdom have excited an alarm as to everything which can tend to equalize the powers of man and have induced some excellent and well-intentioned individuals to adopt ideas as distant from truth and polity as the ideas of jacobinism.
>
> Sir Thomas Bernard, *Of the Education of the Poor* (1809) 4–5.

In France, the Revolution concentrated attention upon the state's responsibility in education. Robespierre asserted: 'The nation alone has the right to bring up its children; we cannot confide this trust to family pride and individual prejudice.' In 1793, Robespierre's Education Bill introduced free, compulsory education for boys and girls. Although little was achieved in practice, education was widely discussed, and interest in French ideas was reflected in English writing in the second half of the eighteenth and early years of the nineteenth century. The economist, Adam Smith, wrote:

> Though the State was to derive no advantage from the instruction of the inferior

> ranks of the people, it would still deserve its attention that they should not be altogether uninstructed. The State, however, derives no inconsiderable advantage from their instruction . . . In free countries where the safety of government depends very much upon the favourable judgment which people may form of its conduct, it must surely be of the highest importance that they should not be disposed to judge rashly or capriciously concerning it.
>
> Adam Smith, *Wealth of Nations* (1776) Book V, chap 1, art 2.

William Wordsworth, who visited France as a young man twice between 1790 and 1792, still wrote in middle age of the State's responsibility towards education:

> O for the coming of that glorious time,
> When prizing knowledge as her noblest wealth
> And best protection, this imperial Realm
> While she exacts allegiance shall admit
> An obligation on her part to teach
> Those who are born to serve her and obey:
> Binding herself by statute to secure
> For all the children whom her soil maintains
> The rudiments of letters, and inform
> The mind with moral and religious truth
>
> W. Wordsworth, *The Excursion* (1814) Book IX, 293–302.

Here Wordsworth asserted that the State should realize the value of knowledge and recognize its obligation to provide for education by statute, a step which it was not to take until the passing of the Elementary Education Act of 1870. The social value of universal education was also stressed in articles in the *Quarterly Review* and the *Gentleman's Magazine*:

> National education is the first thing necessary. Lay but this foundation and the superstructure of prosperity and happiness, which may be erected, will rest upon a rock; lay but this foundation, poverty will be diminished and want will disappear in proportion as the lower classes are instructed in their duties for then only will they understand their true interests; they will become provident, and the wages of labour may be greatly advanced to the unequivocal benefit of all persons; thus will the poor rates be diminished, and thus only may they be ultimately abolished.
>
> *Quarterly Review* VIII (1812) 354.

In a society experiencing the problems of industrialization and urbanization, universal education seemed to promise social stability and an escape from the excesses that had radically damaged France. To those who felt that the enthusiasts for education were 'entertaining French principles', tracts were addressed. They were written by Hannah More who, with her sister, struggled against prejudice and ignorance to educate both children and adults in the industrial centres of the Mendip Hills. The tracts, selling at a halfpenny each, had an enormous circulation and expressed their views in forceful language. In their desires to put fears at rest, they reflect the attitudes towards the class structure which persisted throughout the nineteenth century. The tract written by Thomas Pole in defence of lower-class education is typical of many:

Some Objections to instructing the Poor considered

> An argument has been used in less enlightened periods than the present, which is not yet removed from the lips even of some from whom we might reasonably have expected a greater degree of penetration—that the system of education, so extensively diffusing amongst the poor of the present day, will have the injurious tendency of placing them above their stations in life; and an opinion is actually cherished that, becoming dissatisfied with their condition, there will not ultimately be found servants to undertake the menial, domestic, and commercial employments; but that, aiming to be equal with their masters and mistresses, and excited by human pride, there is a danger of their attempting to throw off all subordination to their superiors.
>
> We should naturally have supposed that no person capable of reflecting on the nature of human society, and the mutual dependence of the several ranks and classes upon each other, could possibly for a moment entertain a fear of this kind; for were men of the most splendid talents to form themselves into societies, professedly to effect such a destruction of right order, or a civil equalization of mankind, others of inferior capacities might laugh at their folly, and ridicule so absurd, so chi-merical a project. The reciprocal dependence of the poor upon the rich for their support, and of the rich upon the poor for their labours, must, through all progressive improvements, absolutely and necessarily exist; and the duties which the several classes owe to each other, will be more conscientiously regarded than could be expected in a state of ignorance and vice. Let the individuals who have indulged these gloomy apprehensions, take a look at Scotland, where the poor (in the Low-lands) are more extensively educated than what is at present anticipated in this part of the country—let them see whether

the knowledge of letters has produced those baneful consequences; on the contrary, does there not exist a more cheerful submission amongst the poor, to those in the higher walks of life; more industry, more economy, more contentment; and are they not also more trust-worthy, because less ignorant, and consequently less criminal, than the poor of England?—Being educated, they are capable of reading, and acquiring an enlargement of mind, which qualifies them to form a clearer judgment of men and things, and more justly appreciate the moral character. I have never understood that pride is more prevalent in the poor of Scotland, than of England; it is the mean offspring of ignorance: ignorance of ourselves—ignorance of true religion, of which humility is one of the strongest characteristics; and the knowledge of the sacred Scriptures, that fountain whence we draw religious instruction, should ever go hand in hand with all our plans for instilling knowledge. When the precepts of virtue and morality are implanted in the minds of the poor, especially if cherished by good examples in the rich, we shall certainy have nothing to fear from the education of our servants, and of the mass of labouring poor.

T. Pole, *A History of the Origin and Progress of Adult Schools* (1814) 56–7.

The efficacy of education for the upper and middle classes was not in doubt, but the need for a literate working-class was less apparent. In spite of rapid changes in the economy almost every job could be learnt while working. A literate man would not necessarily advance more quickly in his occupation than an illiterate man; educated manpower was not at a premium at the end of the eighteenth century. The appeals for universal education rested on the social rather than the economic value of education. If the poor were educated they might make less demands on poor relief, and the poor rate might be reduced. Inquiries made into the condition of the prisons showed that most criminals were illiterate. It was thought reasonable to expect that money spent on education could be saved in a few years from the expenses of criminal justice. It was felt that education would improve morals and there would be fewer outbreaks of violence to disturb the social order.

Few who supported the spread of education were prepared for a radical change in the social order. The letters of Hannah More in explaining her aims in establishing schools in the Mendips well reflect this view:

Let the men and women of Shipham and Rowbarrow become honest and good graziers and hoglers. They were placed in this spot by Almighty direction. The very ground you walk upon points out your daily labour. Excel in that, and an honest hogler is as good in the eyes of the Almighty as an honest squire.

Therefore we wish to recommend you to do your duty in that state of life where God has placed and called you. Every disposition to rebellion against the higher powers would prove how little you are changed in your hearts after all that has been done for you; and remember that rebellion against rulers first brought on the troubles in France.

R. Brimley Johnson, *Letters of Hannah More* (1925) 183.

Pestalozzi, the influential educational thinker, did not see social advancement as an educational end and spoke in the same vein:

Far from believing that one should lead the children of an institute for the poor outside the boundaries of their social position and conditions, I believe it an essential requirement that in it they be made continually conscious of their poverty and their real situation and that they be forced to accept all the exertions and efforts peculiar to their class.

Quoted, M. R. Heafford, *Pestalozzi* (1967) 82.

Opportunities for education for the poor were limited, not only by the meagre nature of the provision, but also by the lack of leisure for both adults and children. In town and country, hours of work were long, and the only day of freedom for most workers was Sunday. To exploit this one free day for education, Sunday schools were started. One of the earliest met at High Wycombe in Buckinghamshire in 1769 when Hannah Ball, anxious that the children should be able to read the Bible, began to teach them the elements of education. The Sunday school movement became a national movement rather than a series of isolated efforts when Robert Raikes, the proprietor of a Gloucestershire newspaper, opened schools on Sundays for the children who worked during the week in the pin factories of Gloucester. He publicized his work, stressing that he hoped by education to remedy indiscipline and illiteracy.

The concentration of illiterate men, women and children in the towns under insanitary and uncomfortable living conditions, from which there was little chance of escape, brought social problems into the open. Raikes had first realized the problem in Gloucestershire:

One day in the year 1780 Mr Raikes decided to go into the lower part of the town in search of a gardener. The man was not in, and Mr Raikes was waiting about. Nearby in the street a score of boys were playing 'check'. The noise was deafening, the oaths were terrible! Mr Raikes was amazed. Turning to a decent-looking woman in a doorway, he expressed his surprise and pain at what he had heard and seen. She replied, 'Ah, sir, that's nothing. We have it so every day. But Sunday is worse. On Sunday the pin-factory yonder isn't working, and so there's more children in the streets, and, sir, then it's like hell!'

These words to the good Sabbath-fearing heart of Mr Raikes came as a shock, and the facts before his eyes were a vivid illustration of the words. 'Something must be done,' said this practical man to himself. But what? Pondering a little, he hit upon a new idea—new to him, at any rate; and new to the world. The idea was to gather these and such like children into schools on Sundays . . .

J. J. Wright, *The Sunday School, Its Origin and Growth* (1900).

Raikes described the way he went to work together with the Revd Thomas Stock, Headmaster of Gloucester Cathedral Choir School:

I then enquired of the woman, if there were any decent well-disposed women in the neighbourhood who kept schools for teaching to read. I presently was directed to four: to these I applied, and made an agreement with to receive as many children as I should send upon the Sunday, whom they were to instruct in reading and in the Church Catechism. For this I engaged to pay them each a shilling for their day's employment. The women seemed pleased with the proposal. I then waited on the clergyman before mentioned, and imparted to him my plan; he was so much satisfied with the idea, that he engaged to lend his assistance, by going round to the schools on a Sunday afternoon, to examine the progress that was made, and to enforce order and decorum among such a set of little heathens.

J. H. Harris (ed), *Robert Raikes, A Man and his Work* (1899) 305.

Many public-spirited people who established or supported Sunday schools looked for the social improvements that were claimed for the Sunday school at Gloucester:

The good effects of Sunday schools established in this city are instanced in the account given by the principal persons in the pin and sack manufactories, wherein great reformation has taken place among the multitudes whom they employ. From being idle, ungovernable, profligate and filthy in the extreme, they say the boys and girls are become not only cleanly and decent in their appearance, but are greatly humanised in their manners—more orderly, tractable, and attentive to business, and, of course, more serviceable than they ever expected to find them. The cursing and swearing, which used to form the sum of their conversation, are now rarely heard among them.

Ibid, 303–5.

This aim was sought, not only by religious instruction in the Sunday school itself, but also by associating the children very closely with the worship of the church to which the school was attached. As had been done previously for charity school children, galleries were built in many churches to seat the Sunday school children at the services; and the regulations for the children of the schools of St John's Chapel, Bedford Row, London, were by no means untypical:

> 3. Silence and reverence must be observed every moment they are in the house of God. There must be no whispering, talking, nor disturbance of any kind. Every little noise in the scholars' gallery disturbs the congregation in the gallery below. The first offence is published by the forfeiture of all the tickets of approbation which the scholar may have then received. The second offence is punished by expulsion from the schools.
>
> 4. Each scholar is expected to come straight from home to the chapel, and to go directly home after divine service is ended, with quietness and good behaviour. All playing and rudeness in the streets on a Sunday, is disgraceful and sinful. The first offence is punished by the forfeiture of all the tickets of approbation the scholar may have then received, and for the second offence the punishment is expulsion.
>
> 5. *Boys* and *girls* are never to be seen walking together on a Sunday to or from the chapel.
>
> 6. They are expected to pay cheerful and constant obedience to the superintendants, master and mistress, and such persons as the master and mistress may appoint to assist in keeping order and silence in their galleries.
>
> Sir Thomas Bernard, *Of the Education of the Poor* (1809) 285.

As the Sunday school movement spread, men and women from all walks of life became interested in the work. Many industrialists and landowners gave financial support, while humbler people offered their services as teachers. Some received payment, but many gave their services voluntarily. Martha More described two working men who gave up their only free day of the week to teach in her school:

> The spiritual improvement of the parish was left entirely to the care and management of Tommy Jones and Johnny Hart, as the two young miners were called, but a Higher Power not only presided over, but greatly blessed these two poor youths, who are concealed from all human sight in the bowels of the earth six days out of seven, and on the seventh day they emerge, like two young apostles, to instruct and enlighten the rising generation.
>
> Martha More, *Mendip Annals* (1859) 2nd ed.

Such enthusiastic teachers did more for their children than teaching them to read. In poor districts, the want and neglect from which the children often suffered led the teachers to act towards them as if they were their parents. Mrs Sherwood, a children's writer, who ran a Sunday school at Bridgnorth in Somerset, wrote in her diary, 'We made bonnets and tippets for our girls; we walked with them to church; we looked them up on weekdays.'

Robert Raikes ensured that the Sunday schools had national support when he founded the Society for the Establishment and Support of Sunday Schools in 1785 with its aim, 'Be diligent in teaching children to read well.' Eminent supporters were John Wesley and William Cowper. The Society worked through local committees on which Churchmen and Nonconformists served together. Ten years later, three-quarters of a million children were members of Sunday schools. The movement now had a national framework, but by 1800 sectarian rivalries had weakened its unity, and individual churches were seeking control of their own schools.

The Sunday school movement made a significant contribution to literacy in the early years of the nineteenth century. When the campaign for parliamentary reform developed, it was able to draw upon the support of many working-class men, who could read its pamphlets, write for the cause and speak at village meetings because of the education they had received at Sunday schools during the previous thirty years. Samuel Bamford recorded that the writings of William Lovett were read on nearly every cottage hearth in the manufacturing districts of South Lancashire. Religious tracts and penny magazines were popular. Newspapers were expensive as they carried a heavy stamp duty which was not finally removed until the 1860s, but so great was the demand for news that working men clubbed together to buy copies of past issues which were often several days old.

For many, the only opportunity to learn to read was provided by the Sunday school. In many areas the Sunday schools extended their activities to provide classes for adults in the evenings. Some children were too young for employment in the factories or fields, others were unemployed and running wild, and so Sunday schools opened on weekdays to try to make use of this free time. At Brentford in 1786, Mrs Sarah Trimmer opened her Sunday school on weekdays to teach spinning to the street arabs. Later she added a knitting school and a school for winding cotton for girls. In the Mendips the More sisters often opened their schools on weekdays to teach knitting and spinning.

This combination of reading and industrial activity had long been considered a desirable education for the poor. Schools of industry dated from 1675 when Thomas

Firmin set up a spinning factory in Little Britain, West
from the age of five and taught them reading and the Ca
well-meaning individuals many schools of industry were
the Prime Minister, supported the idea of a school of i
Cheltenham School of Industry for Girls was founded i
Prestbury, who wrote an account of its aims:

> The object of this charity is to promote religion and
> poor, by early impressing their minds with a just sens
> to their present as well as their future happiness;
> effectually above the necessity of being tempted to s
> enabling them in various ways to earn an honest live ... ng,
> milking, washing, ironing, and every kind of household ... , they are taught to spin, to knit, to sew, to plat whole straw for baskets, to cut out and make clothing, which is afterwards sold to the poor at reduced prices. The school also gives, under certain restrictions, a stated price for work, to any girls or young women who apply for it, and might otherwise, perhaps, for want of employment, fall victims to idleness and vice.

Sir Thomas Bernard, *Of the Education of the Poor* (1809) 220.

This school required that the girls should be able to read before they were admitted as pupils, but a more usual arrangement was for the children to be called out from their work in small groups for an hour or so a day for reading lessons. The hope was that such schools would be self-supporting since the work done by the pupils would be sold to meet expenses, but industrialization took away the market for hand-spun yarn and it was difficult to make the schools economically viable. Even those which concentrated on straw-plaiting met with limited success, and too often the demands of industrial activity severely limited the time spent on learning to read. Few of the industrial schools designed to serve the poorest of the poor lasted for more than a few years.

In some areas the children of the poor might be taught in a charity school. The great philanthropic endeavour of the Society for the Promotion of Christian Knowledge in encouraging the foundation of charity schools throughout Britain had largely exhausted itself by the 1740s. Many schools started in the early years of the eighteenth century were still in existence at the end of the century, but most were inefficient and in decline. A report on a charity school at Harrietsham in Kent in 1837 stated:

> A charity school for girls and boys; reading, arithmetic, writing, and sewing taught.

Under 7, boys 16,
girls 17;
above 7, boys 11,
girls 10.

On Sundays about 15 more. Many of the scholars read fluently, and a few write very fair. Many parents complain they cannot get their children admitted; they pay 1*d.* each. The room is small, not very clean, and badly ventilated.

Central Society of Education (1837) first publication, 357.

Scattered throughout the country were dame schools where, for a small fee, a few pupils were taught, usually by a woman, the 3 Rs and sometimes 'the use of globes'. Some towns and villages had a common day school, usually larger than a dame school, where the pupils were taught by a man. The quality of education in these schools was very variable. When the Central Society of Education made a survey of educational facilities in Kent in 1837 they found a few dame schools of which they could approve, such as that at Boughton Malherbe:

A superior dame's school, consisting of,

under 7, boys 8,
girls 8;
above 7, boys 12,
girls 14.

One penny per week is paid for 37 out of the church-rate, and the parents pay 1*d.* The remainder, the parents pay from 4*d.* to 6*d.* per week. The mistress writes a good hand, and the school apparently is well conducted. She also, with the assistance of her husband, superintends the Sunday school, which is badly attended in consequence of the church being on the confines of the parish; only about 20 children attend. They are paid extra for this by subscription, which averages about 5*l.* per annum. The Clergyman is resident.

Central Society of Education (1837) 356.

The good dame school was probably exceptional, and the survey carried out by the Manchester Statistical Society concluded that the dame schools 'afford no instruction worthy of the name'. Its report on these schools was complimentary neither to parents nor to teachers:

Under this head are included all those schools in which reading and a little sewing are taught. This is the most numerous class of schools, and they are

> generally in a most deplorable condition: the greater part of them are kept by females; but some by old men, whose only qualification for this employment seems to be their unfitness for any other. Neither parents nor teachers seem to consider instruction as the principal object in sending the children to these schools; they seem to regard them rather as asylums for mischievous and troublesome children, than as actual seminaries of instruction, which indeed the superintendents are seldom qualified to render them.
>
> *Central Society of Education* (1837) first publication, 295.

Contemporary knowledge and concern for education in the nineteenth century owed much to the interest of writers like Charlotte Brontë and Charles Dickens. A comparison between a fictional Dame School of Dickens and the report made to the Newcastle Commission by Dr Hodgson shows that, as late as 1859, many of the schools had hardly improved. Dickens wrote of the village evening-school kept by Mr Wopsle's aged great-aunt for youths who each paid her twopence a week:

> The pupils ate apples and put straws down one another's backs, until Mr Wopsle's great-aunt collected her energies, and made an indiscriminate totter at them with a birch-rod. After receiving the charge with every mark of derision, the pupils formed in line and buzzingly passed a ragged book from hand to hand. The book had an alphabet in it, some figures and tables, and a little spelling—that is to say, it had had once. As soon as this volume began to circulate, Mr Wopsle's great-aunt fell into a state of coma; arising either from sleep or a rheumatic paroxysm. The pupils then entered among themselves upon a competitive examination on the subject of Boots, with the view of ascertaining who could tread the hardest upon whose toes. This mental exercise lasted until Biddy made a rush at them and distributed three defaced Bibles (shaped as if they had been unskilfully cut off the chump-end of something), more illegibly printed at the best than any curiosities of literature I have since met with, speckled all over with ironmould, and having various specimens of the insect world smashed between their leaves. This part of the Course was usually lightened by several single combats between Biddy and refractory students. When the fights were over, Biddy gave out the number of a page, and then we all read aloud what we could—or what we couldn't—in a frightful chorus; Biddy leading with a high shrill monotonous voice, and none of us having the least notion of, or reverence for, what we were reading about.
>
> Charles Dickens, *Great Expectations* (1859) chap X.

> . . . none are too old, too poor, too ignorant, too feeble, too sickly, too unqualified

in any or every way to regard themselves, and to be regarded by others, as unfit for school-keeping. Nay, there are few, if any, occupations regarded as incompatible with school-keeping, if not as simultaneous, at least as preparatory, employments. Domestic servants out of place; discharged barmaids; vendors of toys or lollipops; keepers of small eating-houses, of mangles or small lodging-houses, needle-women who take in plain or slop work, milliners, consumptive patients in an advanced stage, cripples almost bed-ridden, persons of at least doubtful temperance, outdoor paupers, men and women of seventy and even eighty years of age; persons who spell badly, most women I grieve to say . . ., such are some of the teachers, not in remote rural districts, but in the heart of London, the capital of the world as it is said to be, whose schools go to make up two thirds of English schools, and whose pupils swell the muster-roll that some statistical philanthropists rejoice to contemplate.

Report on the State of Popular Education in England (1861) Newcastle, III, 483–4.

While enlightened opinion advocated universal education, the voluntary bodies providing the teaching of the rudiments of knowledge to the majority of children were rapidly being overwhelmed by the growth in population. The major provision of education was not only inadequate, but also ill-distributed and inefficient. To provide more education, money and teachers were needed. In 1800 the solution to the problem of establishing cheap and efficient elementary education seemed to have been found. Joseph Lancaster, a Quaker, and Dr Andrew Bell, an Anglican clergyman, demonstrated a method of teaching that harmonized well with the industrial outlook of the time. Their method promised to be cheap and required a minimum of trained teachers. In the monitorial school, older pupils taught younger ones a set lesson which they had learned from the teacher. This was an old device which had been introduced into some schools in the sixteenth century. Bell had used it in the Military Male Asylum in Madras where as Chaplain he had found the boys, the sons of soldiers, receiving little worthwhile education. He dismissed a number of inefficient teachers and replaced them by the older boys. Sand trays were used for drawing and writing. He later made optimistic claims for his experiment:

This system rests on the simple principle of tuition by the scholars themselves. It is its distinguishing characteristic that the school, how numerous soever, is taught solely by the pupils of the institution under a single master, who, if able and diligent, could, without difficulty, conduct ten contiguous schools, each consisting of a thousand scholars.

Andrew Bell, *The Madras School or Elements of Tuition* (1808).

Reading stations in a Lancastrian school,

In London, Joseph Lancaster opened in Borough Road and advertised, 'All who will may send their children to have them educated freely (the expenses of writing books excepted). And those, to whom the above offer may not prove acceptable, may pay for them at a very moderate price.' Lancaster's school thrived, and he was probably driven by the numbers of his pupils to adopt the monitorial system. He probably found some of Bell's ideas worth trying when he read about them in 1800. He experimented with rewards and punishments to encourage pupils and monitors by competition. Lancaster claimed to teach his pupils reading, writing and 'summing' and calculated that the annual cost of education would be 7s 6d per child. He found slates as cheap to use as sand trays. By 1803 he had refined his system and published an account of it:

> The whole school is arranged in classes; a monitor is appointed to each, who is responsible for the cleanliness, order and improvement of every boy in it. He is assisted by boys, either from his own or another class, to perform part of his duties for him, when the number is more than he is equal to manage himself.
>
> The proportion of boys who teach, either in reading, writing, or arithmetic, is one to ten. In so large a school, there are duties to be performed which simply relate to order, and have no connexion with learning: for these duties, different

> monitors are appointed. The word monitor, in this institution, means, any boy that has charge either in some department of tuition or of order, and is not simply confined to those boys who teach. The boy who takes care that the writing books are ruled by machines made for that purpose, is the monitor of ruling. The boy who superintends the inquiries after the absentees, is called the monitor of absentees. The monitors who inspect the improvement of the classes in reading, writing and arithmetic, are called inspecting monitors; and their offices are, indeed essentially different from that of the *teaching monitors*. A boy whose business it is to give to the other monitors such books, &c. as may be wanted or appointed for the daily use of their classes, and to gather them up when done with; to see all the boys do read, and that none leave school without reading, is called the monitor-general. Another is called the monitor of slates, because he has a general charge of all the slates in the school.
>
> Joseph Lancaster, *Improvements in Education* (1806) 37–8.

Lancaster's system of rewards, which showed some understanding of child psychology, was ingenious and used as a constant incentive. Pupils were often given tickets when they deserved a reward, and these were collected to be exchanged for a prize such as a bat, ball, kite or book. Lancaster commented that books with pictures were more in request among the children than other prizes. Punishments were also necessary as some pupils were idle or talkative. Lancaster disliked excessive punishment, but when he felt it was deserved, he again had an ingenious approach:

> Each monitor of a class is responsible for the cleanliness, order, and quietness of those under him. He is also a lad of unimpeachable veracity—a qualification on which much depends. He should have a continual eye over every one in the class under his care, and notice when a boy is loitering away his time in talking or idleness. Having thus seen, he is bound in duty to lodge an accusation against him for *misdemeanor*. In order to do this silently, he has a number of cards, written on differently: as, 'I have seen this boy idle,'—'I have seen this boy talking,' &c. &c. This rule applies to every class, and each card has the name of the particular class written thereon: so that, by seeing a card written on as above, belonging to the first or sixth, or any other reading class, it is immediately known who is the monitor that is the accuser. This card is given to the defaulter, and he is required to present it at the head of the school—a regulation that must be complied with. On a repeated or frequent offence, after admonition has failed, the lad to whom he presents the card has liberty to put a wooden log round his neck,

which serves him as a pillory, and with this he is sent to his seat. This machine may weight from four to six pounds, some more and some less. The neck is not pinched or closely confined—it is chiefly burthensome by the manner in which it encumbers the neck, when the delinquent turns to the right or left. While it rests on his shoulders, the equilibrium is preserved; but, on the least motion one way or the other, it is lost and the logs operate as a dead weight upon the neck. Thus, he is confined to sit in his proper position. If this is unavailing, it is common to fasten the legs of offenders together with wooden shackles: one or more, according to the offence. The *shackle* is a piece of wood about a foot, sometimes six or eight inches long, and tied to each leg. When shackled, he cannot walk but in a very slow, measured pace: being obliged to take six steps, when confined, for two when at liberty. Thus accoutred, he is ordered to walk round the school-room, till tired out—he is glad to sue for liberty, and promise *his endeavour* to behave more steadily in future. Should not this punishment have the desired effect, the left hand is tied behind the back, or wooden shackles fastened from elbow to elbow, behind the back. Sometimes the legs are tied together. Occasionally boys are put in a sack, or in a basket, suspended to the roof of the school, in the sight of all the pupils, who frequently smile at *the birds in the cage*. This punishment is one of the most terrible that can be inflicted on boys of sense and abilities. Above all, it is dreaded by the monitors: the name of it is sufficient, and therefore it is but seldom resorted to on their account. Frequent or old offenders are yoked together sometimes, by a piece of wood that fastens round all their necks: and, thus confined, they parade the school, walking backwards—being obliged to pay very great attention to their footsteps, for fear of running against any object that might cause the yoke to hurt their necks, or to keep from falling down. Four or six can be yoked together this way.

Ibid, 101–2.

In one important respect Bell and Lancaster disagreed in their approach to elementary education. They held different ideas about the sort of religious teaching that should form part of it. Bell, as a clergyman, believed that membership of the Church was an essential part of religious observance and that the children, therefore, should be taught in school the Catechism and other parts of Anglican doctrine. Lancaster, on the other hand, shared the Quaker dislike of dogma and did not think that teachers should try to inculcate their pupils with the beliefs of any single religious body. In his school general Christian instruction and the study of the Bible formed the religious teaching.

At first, however, Churchmen and Nonconformists alike supported Lancaster's scheme. His school seemed to offer a solution to the increasing problem of popular education, and it was widely visited. In 1805 George III received Lancaster and gave a subscription to his work. Yet a month later the harmonious development of the monitorial system ended when Mrs Trimmer published a controversial study of the work of Lancaster and Bell. She claimed that Lancaster had stolen Bell's ideas, and this led to a long, fruitless wrangle between the two men on the origin of the monitorial system. The place of religious instruction in education was also brought to the forefront of the dispute, for Mrs Trimmer condemned Lancaster's work as a menace to the system of Christian education and a dangerous attack on the Church:

> From the time . . . that I read Mr J. Lancaster's *Improvements in Education* in the first edition, I conceived an idea that there was something in his plan that was inimical to the interests of the Established Church . . . I cannot see this 'Goliath of Schismatics' bearing all before him and engrossing the instruction of the common people, without attempting to give him a little check.
>
> Sarah Trimmer, *A Comparative View of the Means of Education Promulgated by Mr J. Lancaster* (1805).

Mrs Trimmer's fears found support among Church people who persuaded Dr Bell to leave his retirement and lead a campaign for the establishment of national schools in which the Catechism and principles of the Church of England should be taught. They wished the cheapness of the monitorial system to be used to the advantage of the Church. One supporter of the idea spoke of 'Dr Bell's intellectual steam engine', which the Church was well-placed to use for it could establish a system of parochial schools which could be manned 'like a line of outworks by the parish clerks raised into respectability by being made parish schoolmasters'.

To further such an aim members of the SPCK in 1811 founded the National Society for the Education of the Poor in the Principles of the Established Church. It opened a school in Baldwin's Gardens, Westminster, where monitors and teachers could be trained and 600 boys and 400 girls taught by Bell's monitorial system. Barrington School, Bishop Auckland, was a similar establishment in the North. The National Society took over many of the charity schools and some Sunday schools and developed them into day schools. Working through the parish and diocesan organization, it had, by 1814, the care of 280 schools and over 40,484 pupils. In 1812 it declared its purpose as follows:

> The sole object in view being to communicate to the poor generally, by means of a summary mode of education lately brought into practice, such knowledge and

> habits as are sufficient to guide them through life in their proper stations, especially to teach them the doctrine of Religion according to the principles of the Established Church, and to train them to the performance of their religious duties by an early discipline.
>
> *National Society Annual Report* (1812) 19.

Lancaster's supporters, led by Joseph Fox and William Allen, organized themselves into a society which became after 1814 the British and Foreign Schools Society. The Society came into existence partly to overcome the problem of Lancaster's incompetence as a businessman and to organize undenominational schools. Within a few years it had opened a number of schools in London and other large towns. Although they were run on Lancastrian lines, Joseph Lancaster himself had severed his connections with them and travelled to the United States and Canada where he opened schools.

The rivalry between the two societies served to promote elementary education and a limited form of teacher training. The sectarian quarrel dominated the development of educational facilities throughout the nineteenth century. The monitorial idea spread widely to America, France, Spain, Italy and Scandinavia, and was still an important method of instruction in the mid-1830s.

While the economy, efficiency and comparative success of the monitorial system seemed to provide a way in which universal education might be achieved, the method had its critics from its early days. These were voiced frequently and were summed up in an inspector's report of 1845:

> We cannot reflect upon the age or requirements of monitors without being struck with the absurdity of expecting any good results from the use of such materials. Taking the average age of monitors, they may be described as boys about $11\frac{1}{2}$ years old, reading with ease, but not much intelligence; writing from dictation, so as to give the sense of a passage, but without any regard to punctuation, or any practical knowledge of grammar; with more or less facility in working the ordinary rules of arithmetic to proportion or practice, but with little or no insight into its principles. The knowledge of geography, history or general information, which the more intelligent of these youths may possess, is not called for in their employment as teachers of the lower classes; and it is hardly needful here to reiterate the severe but just observations which all writers upon our National Schools have made upon the tone and character of the religious instruction under monitors. It is equally prejudicial to the children, who are taught to

confound the holiest things with the least important, and to themselves, since they are thus acquiring or confirming habits either of apathy or irreverence in dealing with those subjects which pertain to man's salvation.

Report of the Committee of Council on Education (1845) I, 163–4. F. C. Cook, HMI, *Report on Schools in the Eastern District.*

2 The need for universal education

In January 1804 the Society for Bettering the Condition of the Poor outlined a suggested inquiry into the existing condition of charity and other schools so as to make possible an extension of educational provision among the poor. It proposed this should ascertain:

> 1. The places in which those schools are entirely adequate to the object;
> 2. The places where a greater extension of their benefits is wanted, and such extension is practicable; and
> 3. Those where new schools for the poor are necessary or expedient.

Sir Thomas Bernard, *Of the Education of the Poor* (1809) 306.

Although the inquiry was never made, it was the forerunner of a device which proved invaluable in the nineteenth century. The scarcity of statistics made it difficult to consider educational needs, but until evidence had been assembled, there could be no action. The century was to bring government inquiries into many of the social problems of the age. One of the earliest was an examination of the working of the Poor Law. With a growing population and the changes brought about by industrialization, the number of people receiving poor relief was increasing. Under the Speenhamland System of poor relief, this had led to a rise in the poor rate in many areas. In 1807 it was calculated that 1,234,000 people out of a population of 8,870,000 were receiving poor relief. The annual cost was £1,267,000.

Philanthropists anxious to help the poor were concerned with living and working conditions in town and country and their effect on society. The Manchester Board of Health founded by the efforts of Dr Percival had recorded some frightening statistics about epidemics and the propagation of illness through the insanitary state of factories. The children of the poor seemed the most helpless victims of the social system, and attempts to help them eventually involved the State in new responsibilities.

Sir Robert Peel Senior was anxious to help workhouse children who were apprenticed at an early age to factory owners and then taken away from their own parishes.

These apprentices had no protection against long hours, low wages and poor living conditions. To save these children from exploitation, Peel introduced the Health and Morals of Apprentices Bill in the House of Commons in 1802. In spite of opposition, this was passed, and in theory these workhouse children were given some protection by State regulation. The Act provided that during some part of the working day, the child employees should be taught the 3 Rs and on Sundays should have some religious instruction and once a month attend church. Although the Act achieved little, since it was difficult to enforce, it at least served as a basis for further legislation and brought the problem forward for discussion.

While Peel concerned himself with workhouse children, Samuel Whitbread, a leading member of the Whig party, adopted a broader approach in a Poor Law Bill introduced into the House of Commons in 1807:

> My wish is not to get rid of the Poor Laws, but I think by taking proper steps they may hereafter become obsolete. The principles in which I would proceed to effect this most desirable object are these: to exalt the character of the labouring classes of the community . . . In the forefront of my plan for the exaltation of the character of the labourer must appear a scheme for general national education. I propose a general system of national education by the establishment of parochial schools; not compulsory upon the poor, but voluntary; and I am confident that it will soon so work its way that every man in England and Wales will, as in Scotland, feel it a disgrace not to have his children instructed.
>
> *Hansard* (1807) VIII, 865.

The educational provisions were only a small part of Whitbread's proposals, and these were eventually transferred to a separate Parochial Schools Bill. For the first time the question was raised in the House of Commons as to whether it was proper for education to be diffused among the lower classes. Whitbread wanted to provide some kind of education for all workhouse children, whether apprenticed to factories or not. He proposed a school in each parish and maintained that the expense of his scheme would ultimately be more than covered by savings in the poor rate.

The discussion made it clear that, if children were to be educated, then they could not at the same time engage in gainful employment. Many voluntaryists felt that this interference with freedom within the family would mean that children would no longer be a financial asset. They realized that compulsion might be necessary to release children from employment for education. The expense of the scheme raised the question of the charitable endowments which Gilbert's inquiry of 1794, in spite of its inadequacies, had shown to be considerable. The view was expressed that education need not be a burden on the State since there were abundant endowments for the purpose if they were properly administered. For many years afterwards attempts to secure financial aid for education from the State were frustrated by this view. Whitbread's Bill was passed by the Commons, but was defeated in the Lords where it was held that 'in schools supported by the nation and supported at its charge, the national religion must be exclusively taught'.

Little had been achieved by legislation, although growing concern for pauper children led in 1816 to an act to prevent the movement of paupers more than forty miles from their own parish. After 1815 most children working in factories had been sent there by their own parents. Sir Robert Peel's bill to stop the employment of children under ten years of age in factories and limit the hours of work of those under thirteen was defeated, but in 1816 a select committee was appointed to inquire into conditions of children employed in the manufactures of the United Kingdom. After it had reported, a further act to limit the working hours of children was passed but, like its predecessors, it was disregarded. It was not until the appointment of four inspectors and the passing of a further act in 1833 that some time for education became a reality for most children.

While the select committee to inquire into the employment of children in factories was collecting evidence in 1816, Henry Brougham, a Member of Parliament and one of a small group of Whigs and Radicals known as the 'Education mad set', urged the appointment of a select committee to examine existing educational provision. Inspired by Samuel Whitbread's work, Brougham determined to continue the struggle for educational provision for the poor. After Whitbread's death, he devoted his dynamic energy both inside and outside Parliament to the task. In a speech at Glasgow university, he proclaimed his aim:

> To diffuse useful information, to further intellectual refinement, sure forerunner of moral improvement, to hasten the coming of that bright day when the dawn of general knowledge shall chase away the lazy lingering mists even from the base of the social great pyramid—this indeed is a high calling in which the most splendid talents and consummate virtue may well press onwards eager to bear a part.
>
> H. Brougham, *Speeches* (1838) III, 95.

Henry Brougham was one of a distinguished group, including Lord John Russell, Lord Lansdowne and Sydney Smith, who went to Edinburgh University during the Napoleonic War and contributed a serious concern for reforming and progressive principles to the political life of the nineteenth century. These Edinburgh students were followers of Adam Smith, supported Malthus's doctrines on population, sympathized with Bentham's utilitarianism and had imbibed the Scottish faith in the power of education. With James Mill, one of their sympathizers, they believed that when everyone could read they would listen to reason, and eventually universal suffrage would bring good government. Brougham's enthusiasm for education was welcomed by James Lindsey, who wrote to Mill in October 1815:

> I am happy to hear that Brougham means to take up two subjects so greatly important as the Laws of Libel and the Education of the Poor. To support a free press and to give the whole mass of the people the capacity of profiting by it is to prepare the triumph of truth and liberty ... God grant him health and vigour, The rest he will command from the energies of his mind.
>
> Quoted in C. New, *The Life of Henry Brougham to 1830* (1961) 209.

Brougham had already been an active member of the Lancastrian Society together with Francis Place, James Mill and other leading Radicals; and in 1816 he persuaded Parliament to set up a Select Committee on the Education of the Lower Orders in the Metropolis. Its main purpose was to gather the statistics which were needed before effective educational measures could be taken. The Committee hoped to examine educational provision for the poor and secondary education in endowed schools with poor scholars. In its report it stated:

> Your Committee have found reason to conclude that a very large number of poor children are wholly without the means of instruction, although their parents appear to be generally very desirous of obtaining that advantage for them.
>
> Your Committee has also observed with much satisfaction the highly beneficial effects produced upon all those parts of the population which, assisted in whole or in part by various charitable institutions, have enjoyed the benefits of education.
>
> *Report of the Parliamentary Committee* (1816).

The inquiries of the Committee were extended from London to the country as a whole, and in 1818 it again reported:

> ... Since the inquiries of Your Committee have been extended to the whole Island, they have had reason to conclude, that the means of educating the Poor are steadily increasing in all considerable towns as well as in the Metropolis. A circular Letter has been addressed to all the clergy in England, Scotland and Wales, requiring Answers to Queries ...

... It appears clearly from the Returns, as well as from other sources, that a very great deficiency exists in the means of educating the Poor, wherever the population is thin and scattered over country districts. The efforts of individuals combined in societies are almost wholly confined to populous places.

Another point to which it is material to direct the attention of Parliament, regards the two opposite principles, of founding schools for children of all sorts, and for those only who belong to the established church. Where the means exist of erecting two schools, one upon each principle, education is not checked by the exclusive plan being adopted in one of them, because the other may comprehend the children of sectaries. In places where only one school can be supported, it is manifest that any regulations which exclude dissenters, deprive the Poor of that body of all means of education.

Report of the Parliamentary Committee (1818) Hansard, XXXVIII, 1207–8.

The Committee stressed the need for government aid in those areas where it had proved impossible by private subscription to raise the money to build a school. Its members also looked at endowments:

The more extended enquiries of your Committee this session have amply confirmed the opinion, which a more limited investigation had led them to form two years ago, upon the neglect and abuse of charitable funds connected with education ... Although in many cases these large funds appear to have been misapplied through ignorance or mismanaged through carelessness, yet some instances of abuse have presented themselves ...

Unauthorized deviations have been made at both Eton and Winchester from the original plans of the founders ... These deviations have been dictated more by a regard to the interests of the Fellows than of the Scholars, who were the main object of the foundation and of the founder's bounty.

Ibid.

Some of the severe social difficulties of the metropolis became more widely known through the publication of the Report. The evidence of the Rector of St Clement Danes Church in the Strand revealed some of the reasons why attendance at school would prove very difficult to achieve:

There are a great many mendicants in our parish, owing to the extreme lowness of some parts of the neighbourhood, and the more children they have, the more success they meet with in begging, and they keep them in that way; so that in the

> weekday we could not get them to a day-school without some different measures were adopted; neither are they fit to appear in them as they are; and on a Sunday they get more by begging than they do on any other day in the week, because more people are out and about; we tried the experiment in several instances, by giving clothes to some of the most ragged, in order to bring them decent to school; they appeared for one Sunday or two, and then disappeared, and the clothes disappeared also . . .
>
> *Ibid*, 14.

The Committee, which included Romilly, Burdett, Brougham and Wilberforce, worked speedily and enthusiastically. It was said of it, 'The government had not learnt the modern trick of making such committees ineffective either by over-weighting them with cranks and obstructionists or using them as an oubliette for shelving some awkward questions.' The Reports contained valuable statistics, and these, together with Lord Kerry's returns of 1833, provided a basis on which educational planning could take place. Some evidence was available concerning the number of children receiving education and the numbers requiring it. Facts were discovered about the distribution of schools, and the attitudes of parents towards the religious training of their children. Brougham was particularly interested in the evidence collected about charitable endowments. He was convinced that educational endowments could be used to supplement the voluntary schemes for educational provision and avoid the need to burden the taxpayer further. His desire to have educational charities soundly administered led to the setting up of a Royal Commission to inquire into the educational charities of England and Wales. The Commission, which sat until 1837, confirmed in its reports Brougham's views that large sums of money were being mishandled and mismanaged. The charity commissioners raised a furore by their activities since they seemed to be conducting a Nonconformist and Radical attack on the Church. It also became obvious that the sheer weight of custom and vested interest connected with charitable endowments made it difficult to apply the money to different causes. Only by legal process through a long and expensive Chancery suit could the purpose of a charity be changed.

When it was obvious to Brougham that it would be difficult to finance popular education from educational endowments, he turned again to Parliament. In 1820 he introduced a bill for the better education of the poor in England and Wales. He had estimated that 3,500 parishes had no school. The bill proposed the provision of parish schools which were to be maintained by rate aid. Feeling that any bill which seemed to take responsibility for school provision from the Church was doomed to failure, he gave the local clergy considerable power in the running of the schools. The bill failed to win the support of either the Church or Nonconformity and was withdrawn. A second bill, introduced by Brougham in 1826, met the same fate.

This lack of enthusiasm for education in the House of Commons arose partly from concern with issues like parliamentary reform which seemed more urgent. Outside Parliament, support for education was not wanting, and voluntary effort mainly directed towards assisting the two societies was producing results. In 1828 Brougham undertook a further survey of educational facilities and found that the number of children attending day schools had doubled since 1818. In some areas, on the other hand, there were school places which were not used. This was shown by the evidence of Robert Owen, a prominent manufacturer with radical educational ideas:

> When I was in Manchester last year there was more school room than children to fill it, and upon enquiring the reason I found that there was such strong inducements held out from the different manufactories of the town and neighbourhood to the parents to send the children early to work that it counterbalanced any inclination such people had to send them to school; therefore the schools were not filled, not nearly so.
>
> *Select Committee on the State of the Children employed in the Manufactories of the United Kingdom (1816)—Evidence of Robert Owen.*

Until the employment of children was effectively limited by law, there was little hope of universal education; but this did not prevent a growing interest in improving methods of education. Other evidence given by Owen to the Committee concerned the curriculum and arrangements of the school which he had established for the children of his workpeople at New Lanark:

> *What is the plan adopted by you?* The children are received into a preparatory or training school at the age of three, in which they are perpetually superintended, to prevent them acquiring bad habits, to give them good ones, and to form their dispositions to mutual kindness and a sincere desire to contribute all in their power to benefit each other; these effects are chiefly accomplished by example and practice, precept being found of little use, and not comprehended by them at this early age; the children are taught also whatever may be supposed useful, that they can understand, and this instruction is combined with as much amusement as is found to be requisite for their health, and to render them active, cheerful and happy, fond of the school and of their instructors.
>
> The school, in bad weather is held in apartments properly arranged for the

purpose; but in fine weather the children are much out of doors, that they may have the benefit of sufficient exercise in the open air. In this training-school the children remain two or three years, according to their bodily strength and mental capacity; when they have attained as much strength and instruction as to enable them to unite, without creating confusion, with the youngest classes in the superior school, they are admitted into it; and in this school they are taught to read, write, account and the girls, in addition, to sew; but the leading object in this more advanced stage of their instruction, is to form their habits and dispositions.

The children generally attend this superior day school until they are ten years old; and they are instructed in healthy and useful amusements for an hour or two every day, during the whole of this latter period. Among these exercises and amusements, they are taught to dance; those who have good voices, to sing; and those among the boys who have a natural taste for music, are instructed to play on some instrument.

At this age, both boys and girls are generally withdrawn from the day school, and are put into the mills or to some regular employment. Some of the children, however, whose parents can afford to spare the wages which the children could now earn, continue them one, two or three years longer in the day school, by which they acquire an education which well prepares them for any of the ordinary active employments of life.

These children who are withdrawn from the day school at ten years of age . . . are permitted to attend, whenever they like, the evening schools, exercises and amusements, which commence as from one to two hours, according to the season of the year, after the regular business of the day is finished, and continue about two hours; and it is found that out of choice about 400, on an average, attend every evening. During these two hours there is a regular change of instruction, and healthy exercise, all of which proceed with such order and regularity as to gratify every spectator, and leave no doubt on any mind, of the superior advantages to be derived from this combined system of instruction, exercise, and amusement.

Ibid.

Owen started his schools before 1813. They were comprehensive in providing for infants, children and adults. He believed that 'man's character is formed for him and not by him', and he preferred activity methods which were similar to those practised on the Continent by Pestalozzi.

Brougham and James Mill studied Owen's methods and in 1818 founded an infant school in Westminster. A second infant school followed at Spitalfields in 1820 under the charge of Samuel Wilderspin, and such was the interest in the education of young children that the Infant School Society was founded in 1824 to establish schools for the children of the poor throughout London.

With the restoration of peace in 1815 travel to Europe made it possible for English educationalists to study European experiments. On the Continent the teaching of Pestalozzi, De Fellenberg and Father Girard were widely discussed, but little was known of their ideas in Britain. While many Continental educationalists were anxious to study the English national system which promised a cheap means of overcoming the problems of illiteracy, a few English men and women went to the Continent. One of the first was Dr Bell, who said of Pestalozzi and his work at Yverdun, 'If he were to dismiss four fifths of his masters, retaining three, and to adopt the monitorial system and the classification of a Madras school, with the emulation, he would be superexcellent.' (R. Southey, *The Life of the Revd Andrew Bell*, 3 vols (1844) III, 94.)

He visited Hofwyl and found De Fellenberg 'a man of much ingenuity and like his master, Pestalozzi, a determined enemy to emulation'; but Father Girard at Fribourg was far more sympathetic to his own ideas:

> There I found the new schools in a most flourishing state: and Père Girard, a priest, who deserves to be recorded in history as an amiable, benevolent and indefatigable friend of humanity and of youth, has the superintendence of these schools. Where one expects least, is often found most. The liberal father felt the true spirit of the Madras system and has introduced none of the fooleries, absurdities, noise and nonsense, which are found in the other schools or in the [Lancastrian] models from which they are chiefly taken.
>
> *Ibid*, 96.

If Bell showed little appreciation of new ideas, others were more perceptive. Owen visited Yverdun, where he was interested in Pestalozzi's sense-training and lessons in mental arithmetic and he was so impressed by De Fellenberg's work at Hofwyl that he sent his sons there to be educated.

A small group of English teachers went to Yverdun to work and learn Pestalozzi's methods. James Pierrepoint Greaves first published the ideas of Pestalozzi in English in *Letters on Early Education addressed to J. P. Greaves, Esq.* (1827). The Mayos, Charles and his sister, Elizabeth, opened a school at Epsom, wrote textbooks and founded the Home and Colonial Infant School Society, which established a 'Model School' for children between the ages of two and ten who benefited from activity methods and a wider curriculum than that followed in the National Schools. It also established a 'Training Establishment' and described its general aims as:

> To obtain individuals of character and piety, and to qualify them, by appropriate instruction, for masters and mistresses; to afford existing teachers the means of improvement, and to recommend them to schools as occasions might offer; to appoint inspectors to visit existing schools; to circulate information on the Infant School system; to print and publish proper lessons; to provide school materials; and to correspond with friends of infant tuition in different parts of the world.
>
> *The Quarterly Educational Magazine and Record of the Home and Colonial School Society* (1848) I, 3–4.

Brougham also travelled widely on the Continent, and his opinion was that 'England in this most essential particular [education] was so far behind other countries'. He was particularly impressed by the work of De Fellenberg for the poor at Hofwyl and wrote several articles describing his methods.

In 1836 the Central Society of Education was founded to publish papers on educational experiments and to serve as a platform for the discussion of the nature and purpose of education. One of its earliest papers described in detail De Fellenberg's method's of teaching:

> The following is a slight sketch of some of the plans adopted by M. de Fellenberg, in Switzerland, in the instruction of the peasantry. A large room, containing all the natural productions of the surrounding country, collected by the children themselves, is a novel feature in a school. But it is the adaption and classification of the different objects to the instruction of those to be taught, that is so peculiarly interesting ... To give a habit of accurate observation—a habit of pausing to survey different objects,—is one of the points most particularly aimed at in the cultivation of the intellect by the founder of Hofwyl. In order to give an idea of his method of doing so, I will give the substance of a few notes taken in the school-room itself while the children were receiving their morning lessons. A boy brings a flower.
>
> *Master.*—What is this? Is it a stone? Perhaps it is an animal?
>
> *Boy.*—No, a plant.
>
> *M.*—Is it a complete, a whole plant?

B.—No, it has not any roots.

M.—What's this? (showing him the stalk.)

B.—The stalk.

M.—What is its colour?

B.—Green.

M.—What is its form?

B.—Round.

M.—What are these? (showing the angles around it.)

B.—Edges.

M.—What is this at the top of the stalk?

B.—A flower.

M.—What is its colour?

B.—Yellow.

M.—And on the sides?

B.—Leaves.

M.—What is the form of the leaves?

B.—The form of a tongue.

M.—Are they smooth or rough?

B.—Rough.

M.—Have they stems?

B.—No.

M.—Repeat the account you have given.

B.—It is a part of a plant, the roots being wanting; with a stalk that is green, round, and with edges: it has a yellow flower; and its leaves are in the form of a tongue, rough, and without stems.

M.—What are these?

B.—Buds.

M.—What are buds?

B.—The flower before it comes to maturity.

The master then proceeds with the leaves of the flower, the petals, the height of the plant, the soil it grows in, the time of the year it appears, its properties, medicinal, poisonous, nutritious, &c.

Thus in one lesson the boy will become acquainted with one flower; in the second, another; in the third he will be made to remark the differences between them, and what they have in common. In the same manner will different objects be proceeded with,—stones, trees, animals, &c. &c. All affirmatives with regard to an object are noted, and a repetition of the sum of them always required. Thus, the observation, discrimination, and memory are exercised at the same time, and not the memory at the expense of the understanding.

Central Society of Education (1837) Vol I, 204–5.

Attracted by the writings about Hofwyl and inspired by Brougham's enthusiasm, Lady Noel Byron, the widow of the poet, visited Hofwyl and on her return founded a school for twenty poor boys at Ealing Grove. She instructed the teacher, Atlee, in De Fellenberg's methods and ideas. The pupils studied a wide curriculum including history, music and scripture as well as the 3 Rs and spent part of each day in manual work either in the gardens or the workshops. The school was acclaimed for its high academic results, its successful manual work and the moral training received by the pupils. As a pioneering school, where new ideas were successfully tried, Ealing Grove School, which lasted until 1852, had a considerable influence, and several other agricultural schools were opened. In England, as on the Continent, educational innovations demonstrated an alternative to the monitorial system and promoted discussion about methods of teaching as well as provision of schools.

By the 1830s a more liberal spirit had taken effect in England. This led to the relaxation of the Combination Acts, the reform of the criminal code and the passing of the Catholic Emancipation Act and culminated in the Parliamentary Reform Act of 1832. Feeling that the reformed House of Commons would appreciate the need for popular education, John Arthur Roebuck, the Radical member for Bath, introduced far-reaching proposals for the consideration of the House. Urging the need for all the people to be enlightened, he suggested:

> When considering any system of education, we must carefully divide from each other: first, the subject-matter of education; second, the various machinery by which this instruction is afforded; and, third, the supervising and contending authority which regulates the whole ... The first great innovation I would strenuously recommend is to make the education of the children no longer dependent on the mere will of the parents and guardians. I would make it a matter of necessity—in order words, would pass a law, making it an offence to keep a child from school between certain years of age ... I would oblige by law every child in Great Britain and Ireland from perhaps six years of age to twelve years of age to be a regular attendant at school. If the parents be able to give and actually do give their children elsewhere sufficient education, then they should not be compelled to send them to the national school. If, however, they should be unable or unwilling to give them such instruction, then the State should step in

and supply this want by compelling the parent to send the child to the school of the State. I consider this compulsion absolutely essential to the success of any general scheme of education . . .

And now first as to the subject-matter of instruction. Although the State determine that every child should receive some instruction, it does not thereby declare that the instruction to all should be alike . . . In infancy all children, no matter what may be their after-destination in life, require the same treatment. All that we can do in that tender age is to provide for the development of the body, prepare the mind for culture and lay the foundation of habits of application and self-government and kindly sympathies. For as regards moral training, this age is all important; as regards the mental, comparatively less so. But inasmuch as all require the same moral training, so the training by which alone those virtues can be produced ought to be extended to all . . .

After the age of infancy is past, and it becomes necessary to convey instruction consonant to the condition of the receiver, then we must take into consideration the necessities which that condition involves. In the present state of society, however, there are certain instruments to the acquirement of knowledge which are deemed so to facilitate its acquirement, that to all alike these instruments are imparted—namely: reading and writing and the element of numbers . . . At the present it seems very generally believed that a rough sort of knowledge of reading and writing is sufficient for a poor man. This is a great—a fatal error. Whilst reading is difficult it cannot be made a means or instrument of knowledge . . . It is, in fact, the foundation stone—if it be not thoroughly secure at first, all future additions will be useless. And the practical conclusion is, that if we do really undertake the instruction of the people, the most complete use and facility in the exercise of these important instruments should most religiously be imparted . . . All that I have hitherto spoken of may be called Primary Instruction and should be alike in all. So far education is the same for the rich and the poor—the ploughman and the philosopher—the maker of pins and the maker of laws. When actual knowledge beyond this comes to be imparted, then comes a consideration of the future destination of the scholar. Any comprehensive system of education would contemplate and include all classes, and for that purpose a series of schools would be adopted rising from infant schools to the all comprehensive university. But in the present state of the public mind this is more than I dare contemplate.

Hansard's Parliamentary Debates, Vol XX, 3rd series, 152–66.

Roebuck's proposals included a trained teaching profession whose members would be respected and protected in old age from want. He planned an educational system organized by districts controlled by elected committees which he expected to provide four types of schools—infant schools, schools of industry, evening schools and normal schools for training teachers. A cabinet minister would control the whole national system which would be financed by school pence, existing educational endowments and taxation. These ideas foreshadowed many of the educational developments which were to take place later in the nineteenth and twentieth centuries. When they were discussed by the House of Commons, it was apparent that members no longer questioned the need to extend educational provision rapidly, realizing that extension of the franchise made this imperative. There was, however, considerable disagreement about the control of education, and especially as Roebuck suggested it should lie with the State. The motion was not pursued, but a few days later when the Report of the Committee of Supply was read, the sum of £20,000 had been provided for education. The money was to supplement private subscriptions for the erection of schoolhouses. The government did not accept responsibility in the direction of education, but paid the grant to two societies, the National Society and the British and Foreign Schools Society to develop their work. The Treasury laid down certain conditions for the grant, and these showed concern and awareness of the inadequate educational provision in many towns. In considering applications for a grant priority was given to proposals from large towns and to plans for schools to accommodate more than 400 pupils. Although some provision in the towns followed the grant, little was done to help the poorer, sparsely populated country districts. In 1834, 1835 and 1838 the government held inquiries to assess the progress and the problems of increasing educational provision. The evidence of witnesses showed the difficulties arising from the denominational issue and concern over the quality of education. One of the most controversial issues was the relationship between the state and the voluntary bodies. Brougham, by 1834 Lord Chancellor and still an ardent enthusiast for education, expressed views which were shared by many:

> *Do you consider that the aid or interference of the Legislature is required for promoting general education in this country?* I am of opinion that much good may be done by judicious assistance; but legislative interference is in many respects to be either altogether avoided or very cautiously employed because it may produce mischievous effects.
>
> *Do you think that a system of primary education, established by law would be*

beneficial? I think that it is wholly inapplicable to the present condition of the country, and the actual state of education. Those who recommend it on account of its successful adoption on the Continent, do not reflect upon the funds which it would require, and upon the exertions already made in this country by individual beneficence.

But if the State were to interfere, and obliged every parish to support a school or schools sufficient for educating all children, two consequences would inevitably follow; the greater part of the funds now raised voluntarily for this purpose would be withdrawn, and the State or the rate-payers in each parish would have to provide schools for 2,000,000 of children, because the interference would be quite useless, unless it supplied the whole defect, which is the difference between schools for one-tenth, the present amount, and schools for one-seventh, the amount required to educate the whole people. Now, to establish and maintain such a number of schools, would be a most heavy expense.

Report of the Parliamentary Committee on the State of Education (1834) 220.

If the government was unwilling to undertake responsibility for a national system of education in 1833, it did extend education, as the result of regulations, to two groups of children—those in factories and in workhouses. The Factory Act of 1833, while limiting hours of employment, appointed inspectors not only to ensure that children under nine years of age were not employed, but also to see that children aged nine to thirteen years attended school daily for two hours on six days a week. Where there were no schools for the children to attend, factory owners had to provide them.

The release of children part-time from their employment so that they might have some education was a device which lasted until 1918 in England and Wales. The problem of the 'half-timers', as they became after 1844, was a difficult one, not only for the pupils, but also for the teachers in the schools:

They are dirty and labour-soiled, in ragged and scanty clothes, with heavy eyes and worn faces. In the clothing districts, their faces, necks and hands are deeply stained with the blue of the dye used for the cloth. From the spinning mills they come covered with the 'flock' or as it is termed the fluff of the yarn—their hair thickly powdered with it—tangled, especially that of the girls, as if no comb could ever penetrate it . . . I fancied, perhaps wrongly, that there was little notice taken of them in the business of the school . . . The master professed himself unable to include them in the various classes without materially injuring progress of the other children.

Inspectors' Minutes, 1844.

The half-time system was the first state-enforced system of education. Until 1870, the educational attainments of some of the half-timers who attended school regularly were superior to those of full-time pupils who attended irregularly.

In 1834 the New Poor Law changed the way in which poor relief was given. Groups of parishes were united to form unions, and the poor who needed relief had to attend the union workhouse. The harshness of the new scheme, which ended most outdoor relief, brought great distress. The problem of the children dependent on parish relief became more obvious with their concentration in the workhouses. By 1839 there were more than 45,000 children, often orphaned, abandoned or children of criminals, living in the workhouses. Among the Assistant Commissioners, whose task it was to organize the new unions, were men like Dr James Kay (later Sir James Kay-Shuttleworth) and E. C. Tufnell, who believed that education could ultimately prevent delinquency and crime. Kay wrote in 1838:

> Whether the state acknowledges its interest in the education of the masses or not, the consequence of the neglect of the pauper class evidently was prolonged dependence and subsequent chargeability as criminals in the prisons and penal colonies.
>
> [Before 1834] the children in workhouses were neither taught nor trained; they were usually placed under the care of an elder pauper, frequently himself unable to read or write, who was directed to look after them, and whose duties consisted in preventing the children from committing acts of mischief. So soon as the children reached the proper age, they were bound out as apprentices—always out of their own parishes—with a considerable premium, and thus the main object of the parochial authorities was obtained, the getting rid of the burden.
>
> *Report of the Poor Law Commissioners on the Training of Pauper Children* (1841) App IX, 341–3.

In *Oliver Twist*, published in 1839, Dickens described the education and apprenticing of young Oliver, who received no training for a trade in the workhouse. Dickens supported Kay's view that the education of paupers should be practical, and he suggested that boys should have industrial training or learn farming and that girls should have domestic training. He tried to touch the consciences of his readers when he wrote of the workhouse children living in 'great, long, rambling wards where a certain amount of weazen life may mope and pine and shiver all day long'; and he deplored 'the utter dullness that begets a hopeless manhood'. Writing in *Household Words*, he supported Dr Kay's plans to open special residential district pauper schools or union day schools away from the workhouses.

One of the most serious problems to be faced in opening workhouse schools was the poor quality of those prepared to accept posts as teachers. Even in a school with over a hundred pupils at Hollingbourne in Kent, the schoolmaster and schoolmistress could give the pauper children little adequate preparation for their future:

> The schoolmaster is about 60 years of age. He was formerly a farmer, lost his money by farming, and set up a village day school. Is now schoolmaster to the workhouse, at a salary of 20*l* per annum, with board and lodging.
>
> The schoolmistress has 10*l* per annum, with board and lodging. She was at one time a pauper, and was subject to a derangement of intellect; she has been in a lunatic asylum, but was discharged as cured. At present the education of both boys and girls is confined to reading and the Catechism; but it is in contemplation to teach the children writing. The girls learn needle-work, but the boys have no industrial employments beyond breaking stones. Fifteen of the boys are old enough and strong enough to go out to work. Mr Elliott thinks there will be no difficulty in disposing of them in the spring. There are only four girls fit to go out to service; and there is a considerable demand for girls as household servants. None of the boys have been apprenticed. The out-fit given by the board for both boys and girls is from 10*s* to 15*s*.
>
> *Central Society of Education* (1837) 358.

The salary and working conditions offered to the workhouse teacher were unattractive, and Kay found that the teachers trained in the model schools in London or in Scotland were not prepared to accept them. Few teachers found residence in a workhouse congenial, and only if they were offered separate apartments and maintenance with a salary of £35 to £40 a year were they prepared to undertake the work. Some of the promising pupils of the workhouse schools were given the opportunity to stay on at school as pupil-teachers. Where the Guardians of the workhouse were enlightened enough to attract staff, an education offering industrial training and teaching literacy could be provided.

One of the poor law schools in which Kay took a particular interest when he became Commissioner of the London district was the school at Norwood. The Headmaster, Mr Aubin, was a well-disposed person ready to experiment with his pupils. Their traditional task had been sorting hair for brushmakers and learning to read and write. The changes suggested by Kay altered the nature of this education:

> Such masters as Dr Kay suggested were engaged; arrangements were made for industrial training; provision was made to secure the happiness and well-being of the poor children in every point of view; and an education was prepared calculated to send them out into the world, not paupers, but active, intelligent, and

good members of society. Four masters from Scotland have been obtained. A tall mast, rigged in due form, which cost 160*l* has been planted in the play-ground, for the purpose of training children as sailors.

Near it is a gymnastic apparatus for the younger boys.

Around the yards are carpenters', blacksmiths', whitesmiths', tailors', shoemakers' shops; in all of which little hands are busily at work, tasking their skill and ingenuity.

There are to be gardens also.

The girls are taught washing and ironing.

The intellectual instruction is of a high character; and the writer knows of no school for the poor, whether out of London or in it, that is so efficient.

Central Society of Education (1839) 287.

At Norwood the 'simultaneous' method of class-teaching was usual with pupils in classes of fifty. For Kay moral education was fundamental, and visiting clergy and the school chaplain supervised religious instruction. He was gratified by the results—'The children appeared happy, confident and ready to work without coercion.' The school at Norwood became widely known and visited. It focused interest on the educational problems of one of the poorest groups in the community.

John Pounds, a philanthropist, began to make provision for children whom no school would accept—the most ragged of children, the verminous, the abandoned, the street arabs. In the 1830s ragged schools were opened by charitable societies or individuals in most large cities. A ragged school was opened in Westminster in 1837 by Mr Walker of the City Mission. He believed that by kind treatment he could draw into the school the poorest children so that he could instruct and feed them. He hoped in this way to save them from a life of ignorance and vice. The desire of many of these neglected children for help is made clear by the author, Thomas Hughes. He wrote of his own time in Oxford in the 1840s, describing a visit paid to a ragged school by Tom Brown:

They turned down a long narrow court in the lowest part of Oxford . . . A group of half-grown lads was playing at pitch-farthing at the further end, and all over the court were scattered children of all ages, ragged and noisy little creatures . . . At the sight of Grey a shout arose among the smaller boys of 'Here's the teacher', and they crowded round him and Tom as they went up the court into the passage of an old tumbledown cottage on the ground floor of which were two low rooms which served as the school-rooms . . .

The crowd of small ragged urchins had filled the room and were swarming on the benches and squabbling for the copy-books which were laid out on the thin desks . . . Soon the smallest were drafted off into the inner room w spelling-books, and the biggest, some dozen in number, settled to ι At last, when the writing was finished, the copy-books cleared a classbooks distributed, the door opened, and two or three big boys c sixteen lounged in with their hands in their pockets and their hats o said they wanted to read with the rest.

T. Hughes, *Tom Brown at Oxford* (1861) 213–14.

Lord Shaftesbury interested himself in the schools and responded to appeals for funds. In 1844, when the Ragged School Union was formed, he became its President, a post he held for forty years. Dickens was one of the earliest supporters of the schools and frequently wrote about them. He approached them critically, regarding them as 'at best the slight and ineffectual palliative of an enormous evil'. He wrote of the Field Lane School, situated in one of the worst criminal areas of London, a huddle of dirty courts and filthy houses made famous as the setting for Fagin's kitchen: 'The school is miserably poor. If they could get a better room (the house they are in is like an ugly drain) above all, if they could provide some convenience for washing, it would be an immense advantage. The moral courage of the teachers is beyond all praise, their office is worthy of the apostles.' (Quoted in P. Collins, *Dickens and Education* (1963) 89.)

Within this hopeless environment, the Ragged School Union tried to meet a multitude of needs:

> There is Scriptural instruction as the foundation, then secular instruction, industrial classes, street employments, refuges, feeding schools, adults, mothers and infant classes, clothing and sick funds, savings banks, libraries and reading rooms, magazines and periodicals, prayer meetings, lectures, ragged churches and emigration.

J. MacGregor, *Ragged Schools* (1852) 22.

Religious and philanthropic effort began to make thinking people aware of the great areas of educational need particularly in the growing towns of England and Wales. Voluntary effort, supplemented by parliamentary grant, led to the founding of many schools, but the rapid growth of the population increased the severity of the problem. It was becoming increasingly clear that a national system of education would need a central administration.

By 1839 the government grant to the two societies had increased to £30,000. The reports of the Committee on English Education in 1838 showed that in the metropolis and the great towns of England and Wales a serious need still existed among the children of the working classes. In spite of the lack of enthusiasm of the Prime Minister, Lord Melbourne, who said to Queen Victoria, 'I do not know why there is fuss about education', those in Parliament concerned with education were determined to create a central administrative machinery. By Order in Council a Committee of the Privy Council was set up in 1839:

LETTER FROM LORD JOHN RUSSELL TO LORD LANSDOWNE

February 4, 1839.

My Lord,

I have received Her Majesty's Commands to make a communication to your Lordship on a subject of the greatest importance. Her Majesty has observed with deep concern the want of instruction which is still observable among the poorer classes of Her subjects. All the inquiries which have been made show a deficiency in the general Education of the People which is not in accordance with the character of a Civilized and Christian Nation.

The reports of the chaplains of gaols show that to a large number of unfortunate prisoners a knowledge of the fundamental truths of natural and revealed religion has never been imparted.

It is some consolation to Her Majesty to perceive that of late years the zeal for popular education has increased, that the Established Church has made great efforts to promote the building of schools, and that the National and British and Foreign School Societies have actively endeavoured to stimulate the liberality of the benevolent and enlightened friends of general Education.

Still much remains to be done; and among the chief defects yet subsisting may be reckoned the insufficient number of qualified schoolmasters, the imperfect mode of teaching which prevails in perhaps the greater number of the schools, and examination of the nature of the instruction given, the want of a Model School which might serve for the example of those societies and committees which anxiously seek to improve their own methods of teaching, and, finally, the neglect of this great subject among the enactments of our voluminous Legislation.

Some of these defects appear to admit of an immediate remedy, and I am directed by Her Majesty to desire in the first place, that your Lordship, with four other of the Queen's Servants should form a board or Committee, for the consideration of all matters affecting the Education of the People.

For the present it is thought advisable that this Board should consist of:

the Lord President of the Council
the Lord Privy Seal
the Chancellor of the Exchequer

the Secretary of State for the Home Department
the Master of the Mint.

It is proposed that the Board should be entrusted with the application of any sums which may be voted by Parliament for the purposes of Education in England and Wales.

J. S. Maclure, *Educational Documents* (1965) 42–3.

The Committee of the Council was the first governmental body responsible for education in England, and it appointed, as its first Secretary, Dr Kay, a man who had already shown by his work as a Poor Law Commissioner that he had a strong faith in education.

3 Training the teachers

Speaking in the House of Commons on 19th August 1847, Thomas Babington Macaulay described candidates for teaching as 'the refuse of all other callings . . . whom no gentleman would trust with the key of his cellar and no tradesman would send on a message. Yet such are the men to whom you trust the rising generation.'

(*Hansard's Parliamentary Debates* (1847) vol 91, 3rd series, 1016–17.)

The monitorial system provided both the National Society and the British and Foreign Schools Society with a way of providing teachers for their schools, and when its defects became apparent, it was difficult to replace. Conditions were not attractive enough to retain more than a few trained teachers in the schools. Most boys left to be apprenticed to a trade; only those who failed took to teaching at the age of twenty-one. The National Society had a model school at Westminster; the British Society sent monitors to the Borough Road School in Southwark for three months' training. But the problem involved status as well as training. A few large schools retained monitors to the age of fourteen or fifteen by paying them small salaries; but most monitors were under twelve and some as young as eight or nine. A school secretary said, 'we much regret that the boys generally leave us at the age of eleven or twelve, or even sooner, and that boys are perpetually leaving us who would make excellent schoolmasters, but we do not know what to do with them'. (*Select Committee on Education* (1843) Minutes of Evidence, 1094–6.)

An answer was found by Sir James Kay-Shuttleworth, who was appointed an Assistant Poor Law Commissioner in 1835. In 1838 the schoolmaster at a Norfolk workhouse fell ill and was very successfully replaced by a boy of fourteen. Kay-Shuttleworth was impressed by this and allowed the boy to continue as an apprentice assistant even after the master returned to duty; thereafter he allowed other work-houses to make similar appointments. Soon afterwards he went to Holland, where he saw how the schools of the Society for the Public Good had adopted a pupil-teacher system, which was an adaptation of the monitorial system enabling the best pupils to remain at school two or three years longer than usual, paying no fees in return for doing some teaching, but able to continue their studies as well. If they proved satisfactory they were recognized as assistant teachers. Kay-Shuttleworth adopted the system as a means of providing teachers in the poor-law schools. Pupil-teachers were apprenticed at the age of thirteen at the poor-law schools at Norwood; they taught during the day and studied in the evening to qualify as poor-law teachers.

When Kay-Shuttleworth became the first Secretary of the Committee of Council on Education in 1839, he was convinced that the weakness of the voluntary schools was largely due to the position and supply of teachers:

> There is little or nothing in the profession of an elementary school-master in this country to tempt a man having a respectable acquaintance with the elements of even humble learning to exchange the certainty of a respectable livelihood in a subordinate condition in trade or commerce for the mean drudgery of instructing the rude children of the poor in an elementary school as it is now conducted.
>
> For what is the condition of the master of such a school? He has often an income very little greater than that of an agricultural labourer, and very rarely equal to that of a moderately skilful mechanic. Even the income is to a great degree contingent on the weekly pittances paid from the earnings of his poor neighbours, and liable to be reduced by bad harvests, want of employment, strikes, sickness among the children, or, worst of all, by the calamity of his own ill health.
>
> J. Kay-Shuttleworth, *The School in Relation to the State, the Church and the Congregation,* ch. III, 'Four Periods of Public Education' (1862) 287 ff.

He sought to remedy this by extending the pupil-teacher system to the voluntary schools, and this was done by the Committee of Council in 1846. He published an explanation of the scheme:

> Your lordships desired to render the profession of schoolmaster honourable, by raising its character, by giving the public recognition of impartially awarded certificates or diplomas, and by securing to the well-trained and otherwise efficient masters a position of comfort during the period of their arduous labours, and the means of retirement on a pension awarded by the Government. They were also anxious to lighten their ill-requited toil in the school by providing them with the aid of assistant teachers trained under their own eyes, and adequate in number to the efficient management of the school.
>
> The arrangements for rearing a body of skilful and highly instructed masters are to commence in the school itself, by the selection of the most deserving of the

scholars who are to be apprenticed from the age of 13 to that of 18. By the regulations determining the character of this apprenticeship, the school is to be in a condition fitting to become a sphere for the training of a candidate for the office of schoolmaster. A great stimulus is thus offered to the scholars to qualify themselves by good conduct and by their attainments for appointment as pupil teachers; to the promoters of the school to render its condition complete as respects fittings, apparatus and the supply of books; and to the schoolmaster so to order the discipline and instruction of the school as to raise it to the proper standard of efficiency.

Kay-Shuttleworth, *The School*, ch III.

The pupil-teacher system marks the real beginning of the teaching profession. It set up standards of good teaching for the first time. It had, however, grave defects. Since classes and staffs were small, pupil-teachers inevitably had to teach the greater part of each day of the week. At first their hours of work were unlimited; only later in the century were they restricted to twenty-five a week. The education they themselves received during their period of apprenticeship was often defective; the head teachers of their school were supposed to help them with their studies, but many were often not skilful or conscientious enough to do this properly. One who was himself a pupil-teacher from 1868 to 1872 wrote:

Many head teachers were unequal to very advanced coaching, and many others had but little energy for anything beyond the ordinary calls of the school. It was quite common for pupil-teachers to take their own instruction after breakfast, say from 7 to 8 a.m., or after the morning or afternoon session . . . Quite 75 per cent of the pupil-teachers received less tuition than they were entitled to.

G. A. Christian, *English Education from Within* (1922) 1–11, 33.

Kay-Shuttleworth had intended that pupil-teachers should complete their course at a training college for two or three years. He himself founded St John's College, Battersea, and his example was followed by societies and diocesan boards of education. The Committee of Council from 1846 awarded a number of 'Queen's Scholarships' to take outstanding pupil-teachers to these colleges, which made it possible for more of them to be built. The first college to be founded by the National Society was St Mark's College, Chelsea, in 1841. The approach taken here towards the training of the students had a considerable effect on the aims and efforts of the colleges founded later in different parts of the country. A feature of St Mark's was its strict discipline as described by one who went there as a student in 1844:

When, at the age of sixteen, I entered St Mark's I found that the gate had closed upon me for five months, and that all my walks and recreation would be limited to the eleven acres which then comprised the College grounds. At that time the Principal's house, with the College Library, the old dormitory and the Chapel, sufficed for the requirements of eighty-six students. In order to obtain permission to leave the College grounds, it was necessary to write a petition in a book lithographed for the purpose, to give reasons minute and particular for the request, and to name the hour of departure and return. Only once in three years—when a dear sister was dangerously ill—did I leave the College during term time. We occasionally went out for walks, but not unattended. We had to walk in double file and in clerical costume; black frock coats, gaiters, tall hats and white ties. But though not allowed to quit the grounds, in order to see our friends, our parents were admitted once a month between two and four in the afternoon. Yet we became accustomed to the rigid discipline and learned to love the place with an intensity which has probably never been equalled since.

Michael Roberts, *Notes on College History 1840–1865* (1946) 26.

Discipline at St Mark's was combined with hard work. The day began at half past five and ended at ten o'clock and included only half an hour set aside for leisure. Eight hours were allotted to 'study and united devotion' and four and a half to 'industrial occupations' among which were housework, cleaning, gardening and looking after cows, pigs and poultry. The services in the chapel were regarded as an important part of the life of the College, and admission was restricted to youths who were baptized and practising members of the Church of England and could obtain the recommendation of a clergyman. The food was plain and served in quantities which were judged sufficient to prevent eating to excess. Behind such an organization of the life and work of the students lay a definite purpose inspired by what was considered to be best-suited for turning the students into the sort of teachers needed in the schools. This purpose was expressed by the first Principal of St Mark's College, the Revd Derwent Coleridge:

The object being to produce schoolmasters for the poor, the endeavour must on the one hand to raise the students morally and intellectually to a certain standard, while, on the other hand, we train them in lowly service, not merely to teach them hardihood and inure them to the duties of a laborious and humble office, but to make them practically acquainted with the condition of that class of the community among whom they will have to labour.

Report of the Committee of Council (1842–3), 297.

This attitude was partly influenced by the social origins of the students. In 1843, the year in which Coleridge expressed his aims, there were forty-six students at St Mark's College; the parents of four of them were described as being in a superior class of life, those of another four were schoolmasters, those of thirteen were labourers, and those of ten were dead, while three had been brought over by a missionary society from Syria to be fitted to teach in Christian schools in their own country. Very different, therefore, from conditions at the public schools and the universities were those offered to these students. It was believed that the poor must be made to work. They were poor, and they were to teach the children of the poor. Discipline must be strict and physical work added to their studies. Subordination, industry and austerity were the principles which governed their existence.

As might be expected, the intellectual standard of those who were admitted to the training colleges was not high. The conditions under which the pupil-teacher system operated meant that even the Queen's Scholars knew very little when they came to college. Their education had been little more than a magnified elementary school course, and many of them do not seem to have learnt much from it. At the same time as the National Society founded St Mark's, it founded, also in Chelsea, Whitelands College for women, and an inspector, reporting on its students, wrote: 'Some of them are exceedingly ignorant, being unable to work the four simple rules of arithmetic correctly; possessing little knowledge either of the Old or New Testament, altogether unskilled in geography, grammar or English history; and utterly unable to spell words of the most common occurrence.' (*Minutes of the Committee of Council* (1847–8) vol II, 500.)

What sort of an education did the students receive in these colleges? Circumstances often did not make this very suitable for them. The colleges were usually short of money, and staffing presented great difficulties. The tutors were not only few in number, but also not equipped to offer the students a useful preparation for their work. In the early days, they were usually clergymen, university graduates and limited in their experience to parochial work or teaching in grammar schools. As late as the time of the Newcastle Commission (1858–61), an inspector said:

> Unfortunately with gentlemen in Orders from Oxford and Cambridge, and tutors not specially educated, the training schools were compelled to use as a means of the students' education such subjects as there were found teachers of. So in one training college classical studies must continue to be employed, and in another mathematical, according as officers of these institutions may happen to have been

educated in the one or other university, or may prefer the one to the other department of learning.

Newcastle Report, 118.

In the 1860s, however, the situation in the colleges gradually improved. The students ceased to come as young as fourteen or sixteen, and now most of them were between eighteen and twenty. Their social standing changed also because a growing number of middle-class families were willing for their children to become teachers. Their standard of attainment improved, though it was still not very high by the mid-1870s, when it was said of the average candidate for admission to a training college:

He can work the ordinary rules of Arithmetic, but not problems involving rules; he can write out a proposition of Euclid by memory, but cannot employ it intelligently; he knows just enough Algebra to be confused; he can parse an English sentence fairly, and he has a very fair knowledge of the bare facts of geography and history; he has a slight smattering of a French or Latin vocabulary; he knows the ordinary forms of schoolkeeping.

Committee of Council Report (1876–7) 685–6.

The staffs, too, of the colleges were improving. It was possible to increase their numbers and appoint tutors who had been schoolteachers and, nearly always, students of the college. The men's colleges were foremost in doing this, but the women's colleges gradually followed their example. An inspector reported on the women's college in 1864:

Two great points have been secured, in the first place all the governesses now employed have 1st class certificates and have been thoroughly trained, with very few exceptions, in the institutions where they are employed. In the next place, a sufficient number of governesses are now employed to do the work thoroughly and without any undue pressure upon their physical and mental powers . . . The best governesses are most willing to overwork themselves. I have cases before my mind in which the work has been done admirably,—while the constitution of the governess was undergoing a process of excitement which, but for timely interference, would have issued in speedy and irreparable exhaustion. In some cases, it has only been by dint of most careful inquiry into the amount of work actually done by the governesses that I have been able to convince the Managers of the importance of increasing the staff.

Committee of Council Minutes (1864–5) 361.

The range of subjects taught in the colleges had by now become amazingly large, especially for the women students who were being prepared to teach the youngest children. An idea of this range may be gathered from an application made by a woman about 1879 for a post as a teacher in an infant school:

> I can teach the following specific subjects paid for as such by the Education Department (Schedule 4, New Code): Mathematics, French, Latin, Physical Geography, Domestic Economy (including Practical Cookery); I can give instruction in Freehand Drawing, Linear Perspective, Model Drawing, Landscape Drawing and Painting in Water Colours; in Needlework and Cutting Out (according to Schedule 3, New Code), in Drill (Calisthenic and Physical Exercises) and in Vocal Music (Old Notation); I also understand the Kindergarten System, the rudiments of German and Italian; and possess a powerful Soprano Voice of more than ordinary compass.
>
> M. C. F. Morris, *Yorkshire Reminiscences* (1922) 126.

Yet what this meant was that the training college course was largely still another magnification of the elementary school course. The future teachers of the children of the poor were equipped with a knowledge of all manner of facts in a variety of subjects, but any suggestion of a wider culture was omitted as unfitted for their purpose. Among those who were dismayed by this was Canon S. A. Barnett, Vicar of St Jude's, Whitechapel, and the founder of Toynbee Hall in 1884. Intellectual narrowness and lack of initiative seemed to him the inevitable result of the way teachers were trained:

> The first step in educational reform is improved training for teachers, and the second is greater liberty for such teachers to use their own methods to reach their own end. Vain is it for anyone to think that by rules and regulations he can secure the real education of the people. Character is the chief element in good teaching, and character is the only product worth considering. When our system is such to establish as teachers men and women who 'think clearly, feel deeply and bear fruit well', men and women who have the power to teach with authority; when we have such teachers, we shall have people able to choose the good and refuse the evil, taught both how to enjoy the world and how to enjoy God.
>
> H. O. Barnett, *Canon Barnett, His Life, Work and Friends* (1921) 350.

Others as well as Barnett came to the conclusion that, because the opportunities of helping the adult practising teachers were so limited, it was more urgent to do something for those still in training and particularly the pupil-teachers, both because their education was more limited even than that of the college students and because they were considerably more numerous. From the outset there had only been enough colleges to take a minority of future teachers, and the expansion of elementary education after 1870 made the position worse. As late as 1902 about 55 per cent of existing teachers had obtained the teaching certificate without going to a training college.

Matthew Arnold had been impressed by the lack of culture produced in pupil-teachers by the system of training and stated in his General Report for 1852:

> I have been much struck in examining them towards the close of their apprenticeship, when they are generally at least eighteen years old, with the utter disproportion between the great amount of positive information and the low degree of mental culture and intelligence which they exhibit. Young men, whose knowledge of grammar, of the minutest details of geographical and historical facts, and above all of mathematics, is surprising, often cannot paraphrase a plain passage of prose or poetry without totally misapprehending it, or write half a page of composition on any subject without falling into gross blunders of taste and expression. I cannot but think that, with a body of young men so highly instructed, too little attention has hitherto been paid to this side of education, the side through which it chiefly forms the character.
>
> Leonard Huxley (ed), *Thoughts on Education from Matthew Arnold* (1912) 5–6.

From the late 1870s several larger school boards sought to remedy the weaknesses in the education of the pupil-teachers by setting up pupil-teacher centres at which they were instructed in central classes, usually in the evenings and on Saturday mornings. The Liverpool School Board established its centre in 1876:

> The premises for the female teachers consist of two private houses, which one of the members of the Board has placed at the Board's service free of rent; the male teachers are accommodated in rooms specially set apart at one of the Board's schools. The subjects taught are arithmetic, grammar, music, history and (for males only) Latin, mathematics, magnetism and electricity, and acoustics, light and heat, and (for females only) the art of teaching, French, domestic economy and animal physiology . . . For facility of their instruction the pupil-teachers are divided into two groups, according as the schools to which they respectively belong are examined in the Spring or the Autumn, and in each group are classified according to the years of their apprenticeship. Out of private funds tea is provided at both centres for the pupil teachers, so that the inconvenience and

loss of time is avoided, which would necessarily occur if the teachers had to go to their homes for this purpose before coming to the classes. Central reference libraries (including a valuable collection of scientific works presented to the Board by a local science committee) have been provided for the pupil-teachers, and a small sum per head per annum is devoted by the Board to their extension. The female pupil-teachers have the privilege of practising on the pianos which are provided for the use of the teacher of vocal music. Omnibus tickets are given from a private source to those pupil-teachers who come from a distance, but only on condition of their regular attendance at the classes.

Second Report of the Royal Commission on Technical Instruction (1884) V, 209–10.

The establishment of the pupil-teacher centres brought considerable advantages for those who attended them. They were better taught by a number of specialist teachers. They were also taught in greater numbers and had opportunities for social intercourse, which gave them a sense of corporate life and broke the isolation in which many of them had lived and worked when they went only to their school. The centres did not, however, remedy all the defects of the pupil-teacher system. The curriculum they studied was unchanged, and they associated only with other future teachers. One of Barnett's friends, P. Lyttleton Gell, the Chairman of the Council of Toynbee Hall, was also concerned about them. He wrote in 1886:

These boys, the teachers of the coming generation of Englishmen, are, in what should be the brightest and freest time of their lives, subjected to a never-ending and monotonous round of cramming and being crammed, and have little chance of seeing anything of the brighter and nobler side of education. They greatly want the friendship of men who have been accustomed to regard the acquisition of knowledge from a more disinterested standpoint, men who can imbue them with something of their own love for literature and science.

H. O. Barnett, *op cit*, 342.

When the Royal Commission on the Elementary Education Acts (known as the Cross Commission) was appointed in 1885, one of the subjects it considered was the training of teachers. Its large and divergent membership prevented it from producing a united report and on this (as, indeed, on almost every issue) the commissioners were divided into a majority and a minority, each group writing its own report. The majority report upheld the pupil-teacher system as there seemed to be 'no other available, or as we prefer to say, equally trustworthy source from which an adequate supply of teachers is likely to be forthcoming'. Nor had it any changes to suggest in the organization of training colleges. It generally accepted that the extension of the two-year course by another year 'would be a great advantage for some students', but would not recommend this because it was not 'yet feasible'. Another suggestion, aimed at broadening the education of some students, it condemned completely:

> It has been suggested that if students were allowed a third year of training, to be spent at Oxford or Cambridge, the benefit would be considerable in completing their equipment for the best class of service in their profession. To any such suggestion the objections seem to us, under existing circumstances, to be very great . . . Such students would be unsettled and unfitted, rather than prepared for their work as public elementary teachers, and this proposal therefore seems to us to be inapplicable to those who are to become teachers in elementary schools.
>
> *Report of the Royal Commission on the Elementary Education Acts* (Cross Report), III, 88, 145.

The minority report took the opposite view on both matters. Its opinion about teachers was that 'the overwhelming mass of the evidence is that these young people are unsatisfactory teachers and ill-taught and ill-trained as scholars', and it considered that 'whether we look at these young people as teachers or as students, they are the most unsatisfactory part of our educational system'. It also stated, 'We think that the other schemes suggested to us of training students in connection with places of higher education deserve a much heartier support than they receive in the report of the majority.'

The minority were to prove right in both these matters. After 1902 it became the aim of the Board of Education to encourage future students to attend a secondary school and to proceed then to a training college, and the number of pupil-teachers began to decline. By 1913 London had none. Several of the pupil-teacher centres were converted into secondary schools. One of these was at Brighouse in Yorkshire, though the report of its first inspection in 1906 shows that pressure had often to be applied to the local authorites to get them to make the conversion satisfactorily:

> When, in 1905, application was made to the Board of Education for recognition of this Centre, the Education Authority at Brighouse expressed its intention to establish a Girls' Secondary School and transfer the Centre to it. Upon this understanding recognition was granted to the Centre to be held temporarily at the Mechanics Institute, and the Board expressed its opinion that these premises were quite unfitted for anything beyond temporary occupation. Up to the date of the Full Inspection no definite step has been taken by the Brighouse Authority towards the erection of permanent premises . . .

> The Centre has the use of two class rooms upon the first floor, both of which have recently been redecorated. Of these one is a long room fitted with antiquated long desks and so ill-lighted that the back of the room is always useless without artificial light, and in the front of the room pupils face such light as there is. The other room behind it and smaller is furnished with new single desks and has good light. In both rooms the noise of passing traffic much interferes with the teaching.
>
> P. H. J. H. Gosden (ed), *How They Were Taught* (1969) 212–14.

The views of the minority of the Cross Commissioners about the association of teacher training 'with places of higher education' also prevailed. In 1890 the Education Department gave recognition which enabled Queen's Scholars to attend the day training colleges which had been established in connection with several universities. These were intended to allow would-be elementary school teachers to obtain their training without having to go into residence in a denominational college. In most of them the students went to the classes and lectures given by the university, but received their training at the day college. One of the earliest of the new colleges was founded for women at Cambridge in 1885 through the efforts of Miss Frances Mary Buss, the redoubtable founder of the North London Collegiate School for Ladies. Its first Principal was Miss E. P. Hughes, one of the most brilliant of Newnham's graduates, and it was accommodated in a couple of small terrace cottages which had been knocked together. Miss Hughes wanted her students to learn something beyond a detailed knowledge of the daily routine of a school class. She regarded education as a subject worthy of study in its own right and wanted to extend the teachers' outlook. One of her first students has described her pioneering work:

> Obviously Miss Hughes had her time cut out. Not being at all satisfied with the kind of training of teachers hitherto in vogue, she had to create the whole curriculum along new lines. Nearly all the tuition was provided by herself. And she had to live in extremely close quarters with fourteen girls, one or two of whom were temperamental, not to use a stronger term. She told us later on that when the task was first proposed to her she refused it flatly, but Miss Buss had pointed out to her that it was a grand opportunity, that she was cut out for it, that there was no one else to do it, and that she simply must. We North Londoners were well able to picture that scene. To this day I am amazed at her pluck. Psychology and logic had been her special subjects at Newnham, and these gave her no trouble, but she had to give us lectures on the history of education, hygiene, speech production, methods of teaching and theories of discipline, and

school management in general, in all of which she was merely feeling her way.

M. Vivian Hughes, *A London Girl of the Eighties* (1936), 124.

In their early years, the day colleges ran into many difficulties. At first they had some students who took a three-year course, reading for their degree and following the educational course at the same time, but many of their students were not capable of doing this and merely followed a two-year course which did not gain them a degree. During the opening years of the twentieth century, however, the day colleges became university departments of education and were able at first to insist that all their students must study for degrees and later to postpone the education course to a fourth, post-graduate year. By that time, training for elementary and for secondary education were being distinguished, and universities were establishing post-graduate secondary training courses. Not until after the First World War, however, did the university departments of education concentrate upon secondary training.

4 Self-help

A static view of society governed the attitudes of many who devoted their energies and money to the education of the poor. Hannah More considered it cruelty to educate a child beyond his station in life. In contrast, Samuel Smiles, expressing his philosophy in *Self-Help* (1859), sought a more dynamic society. He wanted to see the poor progress both socially and economically, and he urged them to rely on their own efforts to lift themselves up:

> Self-help to re-inculcate the old-fashioned but wholesome lessons which cannot perhaps too often be urged—that youth must work in order to enjoy—that nothing creditable can be accomplished without application and diligence—that the student must not be daunted by difficulties but conquer them by patience and perseverance—and that, above all, he must seek elevation of character without which capacity is worthless and worldly success is nought.
>
> Samuel Smiles, *Self-Help* (1859) ch IV.

Smiles, while advocating the view that 'God helps those who help themselves, Go now and do likewise', took a realistic view of the possible effects on society, and he uttered a cautionary note:

> One way in which self-help may be degraded is by regarding it too exclusively as a means of 'getting on'. Viewed in this light, it is unquestionable that education is one of the best investments of time and labour . . .
>
> Self-culture, however, may not end in eminence. The great majority of men in all times, however enlightened, must necessarily be engaged in the ordinary avocations of industry, and no degree of culture which can be enforced upon the community at large will ever enable them—even were it desirable, which it is not—to get rid of the daily work of society, which must be done. But this, we think, may also be accomplished. We can elevate the condition of labour by allying it to noble thoughts, which confer a grace upon the lowliest as well as the highest rank.
>
> *Ibid*, Ch XI.

The industrial and social changes created by the Industrial Revolution brought a desire to read which had not existed to the same extent in a static, rural economy. The Methodist revival of the eighteenth century had stressed individual participation in class meetings, while John Wesley urged the need for literacy among his followers so that they might read the Bible and the hymn-book. The Methodist class meeting, with its pattern of reading and discussion, was imitated by later working-class groups. The incentive to learn to read was encouraged by the growth of popular literature. During the French Revolution, radical political views were expressed in pamphlets addressed to the common man. Tom Paine's *Rights of Man* (1791–2) sold thousands of copies. In many towns and villages the formation of corresponding societies gave urgency to the desire to read. Groups of small tradesmen and artisans in the towns joined together for regular discussion, usually of a political nature. These meetings, often held on Sundays, provided a new form of self-education. Francis Place described the procedure of the London Corresponding Society:

> I met with many inquisitive upright men, and among them I greatly enlarged my acquaintance ... We had book subscriptions, ... and the books for which everyone subscribed were read by all the members in rotation who chose to read them before they were finally consigned to the subscriber. We had Sunday evening parties at the residences of those who could accommodate a number of persons. At these meetings we had readings, conversations and discussions.
>
> Letter of Francis Place (1794) quoted in R. K. Webb, *The British Working-Class Reader* (1955) 36–7.

Discussion ranged widely at these meetings, and it was concern about the political activities of the corresponding societies that led to their suppression in 1799. The government feared sedition from the societies and saw many dangers in the growth of a radical press. After 1815 the clubs revived—literary groups and Hampden Clubs discussing Parliamentary reform—and in many areas small groups of men met together regularly to collect books and pamphlets. On William Lovett, the Chartist leader, the effect of such gatherings was considerable:

> That which first stimulated me to intellectual enquiry, and which laid the foundation of what little knowledge I possess was my being introduced to a small literary association, entitled the Liberals, which met in Gerrard Street, Newport Market. It was composed chiefly of working-men, who paid a small weekly subscription towards the formation of a select library of books for circulation among one another. They met together on two evenings in the week, on one of

Examination of students at the University of Durham, 1842. The engraving shows Bishop Cosin's Library being used as an examination hall. Cosin's Library was founded in 1669 and is still in the same room on Palace Green

> which occasions they had generally some questions for discussion, either literary, political or metaphysical . . .
>
> My mind seemed to be awakened to a new mental existence: new feelings, hopes and aspirations sprang up within me, and every spare moment was devoted to the acquisition of some kind of useful knowledge.
>
> William Lovett, *Life and Struggles* (1876) 28–9.

From these movements to supply the books which working people could not afford, the growth of the free library movement can be traced. And working people, who desired to learn to read, attended Sunday schools with their children, as described by Thomas Pole, a Quaker doctor, who took a prominent part in providing adult education for the poor: 'Some adults of mature age, we are well aware, have been from time immemorial introduced into schools established for the education of children and have acquired that portion of knowledge which has been essentially serviceable to them through the remainder of life.' (Thomas Pole, *A History of the Origin and Progress of Adult Schools* (1814) 2–3.)

Robert Owen at his schools in New Lanark made provision for adults to be educated in the evening, and some of the Sunday schools provided evening classes during the week, particularly for adults who wanted to learn to write, since many schools taught only reading on Sundays.

The opportunities for adults to gain education were limited, and an early attempt to meet the need led in 1789 to the establishment of an institution in Birmingham to continue the education of young men who had completed the normal Sunday school course. Its curriculum included not only the 3 Rs, but also book-keeping, natural science and geography. Classes were held on weekday evenings, and the members, who became known as the 'Cast Iron Philosophers' from their interest in science, established a library for their use.

The first school exclusively for the instruction of adults was opened in North Wales by Thomas Charles, Vicar of Bala in Merionethshire, in 1811, who wrote of it:

> The first attempt succeeded wonderfully, far beyond my most sauguine expectation, and still continues in a most prosperous state. The report of the success of this school soon spread over the country, and, in many places, the illiterate adults began to *call for instruction.* In one county, after a public address had been delivered to them on that subject, the adult poor, even the aged, flocked to the Sunday Schools in crowds; and the shopkeepers could not immediately supply them with an adequate number of spectacles. Our schools, in general, are kept in our chapels; in some districts, where there are no chapels, farmers, in the summer-time, lend their barns. The adults and children are sometimes in the same room, but placed in different parts of it. When their attention is gained and fixed, they soon learn; their age makes no great difference, if they are able, by the help of glasses, to see the letters.
>
> *Ibid*, 3.

The opening of adult schools depended upon the enthusiasm and voluntary work of a few people. In Bristol the efforts of William Smith, a poor, uninstructed door-keeper at the Methodist Chapel, started a movement in 1812 which spread so rapidly that in 1813 Bristol had twenty-one schools for men and twenty-three for women. It began when Smith was asked by a poor man for a Bible, which he obtained from the Bible Society for him through one of its local officials, who also encouraged him to attempt to teach the poor to read the scriptures and promised him the assistance of the Society:

> The heart of Smith was now too full to admit of procrastination; he lost no time; he entered the very next day on this new field of labour, with uncommon industry

and zeal. He selected two friends from among his humble associates, who accompanied him to what is called the Out-parish of St Philip and Jacob, a large proportion of which is inhabited by the poorest classes: this parish they traversed, to take down the names of those who were willing to subscribe small weekly sums for purchasing the Scriptures, as recommended by the parent Society in London, so that they might obtain them at very reduced prices, in preference to gratuitous distribution. Many of those to whom the application was made, observed—'I should be very glad to have a Bible; but it will be of no use to me—I cannot read.'—This afforded Smith an opportunity of asking them whether they would like to learn to read, if a school should be opened? Most, or all, embraced the offer with expressions of pleasure; their names were immediately taken down, and the first man, entered on the list of learners, was William Wood, aged sixty-three; the first woman, Jane Burrace, aged forty. Two rooms, free of expense, were sought for and obtained the same evening; after which two persons, who had been formerly employed in teaching in charity schools for children, were applied to, who readily undertook to conduct the two intended schools—one for men, and the other for women. William Smith still laboured under some embarrassment respecting his future procedure, in procuring books for the use of the scholars: after deliberating some time on this point, he applied to Captain John Richards, of Kingsdown, for the loan of a few, with which to commence the Adult Schools; the Captain furnished them cheerfully, and spoke encouragingly of the undertaking. Notice was now given amongst the poor of the before-mentioned parish, that it was intended to open the proposed schools on the eighth of the ensuing month, only nineteen days from the time Smith first communicated his mind on the subject to Stephen Prust. They were opened at the time fixed—eleven men and ten women being admitted on the day of commencement; the numbers increasing every week, until the rooms were filled.

Ibid, 8–9.

The adult schools spread an interest in education and showed that those who were no longer children could learn. By 1850 about 30,000 people had learnt to read and write through the adult schools, which had now largely completed their limited task. A teacher at a women's school in Ipswich explained this trend:

I am disposed to think that most who require instruction have been taught; the number of scholars who now attend is greatly lessened; we have but thirteen remaining upon the list, but these are regular in their attendance, and the order of the school has not at all decreased; so that it seems to be wearing away in a good old age, having nearly fulfilled the object for which it was established.

Ibid, 12.

Another voluntary movement to educate the working class began in Scotland and spread rapidly throughout the country. At the Andersonian Institute in Glasgow, Dr George Birkbeck, the Professor of Natural Philosophy and Chemistry, visited the workshops where scientific apparatus for his lectures was made. He became aware of the workmen's curiosity about the work they were doing, and he decided to instruct these men in the principles of science if they were interested. Birkbeck explained that the attitude of the men had brought him to this decision, when he found:

> My attention was arrested by the inquisitive countenances of a circle of operatives, and I beheld, through every disadvantage of circumstances and appearance, such strong indication of the existence of the unquenchable spirit and such emanations from the heavenly-hired lamp of man that the question was forced upon me—Why are these minds left without the means of obtaining that knowledge which they so ardently desire; and why are the avenues to science barred against them because they are poor?

J. W. Hudson, *The History of Adult Education* (1851) 33.

Birkbeck attracted an appreciative audience of orderly attentive mechanics, often numbering five hundred or more. In 1823 the Glasgow mechanics wrote to him, and from their letter it is clear that they appreciated his personal qualities as a teacher:

> You formed your scheme of improvement from an intimate acquaintance with human nature. You judged that the apparent mental lethargy of the operatives towards science arose from no infirmity of their mental powers, and you judged right . . . You undertook the generous task of giving the first impulse and of directing their attention to studies worthy of their pursuit.

J. G. Godard, *George Birkbeck, the Pioneer of Popular Education* (1844) 40.

It was not until the 1820s that mechanics' institutes opened rapidly in towns, where their origin can be traced to the enthusiasm of a group of people or sometimes an individual. There was support from industrialists for limited scientific education for the artisan. In Glasgow the Mechanics' Class at the Andersonian Institute broke away to form an independent Mechanics' Institute in 1823 with Birkbeck as a patron. Independence and self-government was a feature of the new body. At Edinburgh, Leonard Horner created the Edinburgh School of Arts to 'provide instruction in the sciences in relation to their application to the arts'. Inspired by the Scottish examples, a Mechanics' Institute was founded in London. It was supported by Birkbeck and many of the leading Radicals, and during the first year lectures were given in astronomy, chemistry, hydrostatics, French and architecture.

The spread of the movement beyond London can be traced from notices in provincial newspapers which indicate local interest:

> The present week has been most interesting in its consequences to the Devenport and Stonehouse Mechanics' Institute. For the first time in this town, and we may truly say for the first time in the west of England, lectures have been delivered to the working mechanics. So great was the demand for tickets, it was judged necessary to erect temporary galleries around the sides of the Town Hall to accommodate the numerous and eager applicants. The utmost order and attention prevailed, and Mr Lloyd, the lecturer, was listened to with the deepest interest.
> *Exeter Flying Post*, 8th September 1825.

The new institutions were linked by the *Mechanics' Magazine*, and effective encouragement and support was given by Henry Brougham, who 'had indeed a passion for educating other people, particularly in mathematical and physical science'. His article in the *Edinburgh Review*, 'Practical Observations upon the Education of the People Addressed to the Working Classes and their Employers', was widely circulated in 1825. In it he advocated lectures on scientific subjects and the creation of book clubs. By 1826 over 104 institutes had been founded. With the growth of the movement, difficulties became clear. Many artisans had little chance of understanding the scientific lectures and experiments since they had no knowledge of elementary mathematics. It was difficult to find lecturers, and many societies were short of the money necessary for their payment. With the growing agitation for parliamentary reform, many mechanics were more interested in political activity then scientific education. A changing membership of shop assistants, clerks and women directed many institutes away from scientific to literary interests. In some areas the pressure of work made attendance at the institutes difficult for many:

> Mr Moncton Miles put a curious question, 'Have you found the literary habits of artisans very much affected by the circumstances of good or bad trade?' Answer, 'Yes, but not to so large an extent as might be supposed. During a period of great depression, two or three years ago, several mechanics' institutes were formed in villages in the West Riding because the working people had time to spare; but as soon as the mills began running full-time again, the institutions were

dropped. The people had simply employed in self-improvement the time that was liberated during the scarcity of employment in the mills.'

Samuel Smiles, *Autobiography* (1905).

Some institutes suffered from mismanagement and declined; others eventually developed into important educational institutions in their own right. The London Mechanics' Institution became Birkbeck College, that at Manchester became a College of Advanced Technology. A number of the mechanics' institutes became technical colleges and made a significant contribution to the interest in and development of scientific education.

The mechanics' institutes gave an impetus to the demand for public libraries. Most institutes had a library or arranged the exchange of books through an itinerant library. By the Act of 1850 local authorities could provide public libraries, and many grew from local mechanics' institutes libraries.

For those working men who rejected the mechanics' institutes or lived in areas where institutes had not been formed, there were coffee houses, over 1,600 in London, mutual improvement societies and public reading rooms. The availability of periodicals and daily papers attracted many readers who were expected to pay a reading fee of a penny.

In 1826 Henry Brougham was the prime mover in the formation of the Society for the Diffusion of Useful Knowledge (SDUK). The Society published cheap primers, textbooks and pamphlets. In 1829 it began to publish regular series. Brougham himself wrote the first articles on *Objects, Advantages and Pleasures of Science*. This was followed by nineteen volumes on scientific subjects. History and geography were included in the *Library of Entertaining Knowledge*. The publishers claimed that in their volumes they printed the contents of 180 octavo pages on 32 octavo pages. Perhaps the best-known publication of the Society was the *Penny Cyclopaedia*. The effects of the activities of the Society were noted by the Parliamentary Committee on the State of Education in 1834:

> The establishment of useful libraries is another object in promoting which the Government may safely and most advantageously interfere. The exertions of the Society for the Diffusion of Useful Knowledge have so greatly reduced the price of books, maps and prints and are so constantly multiplying good elementary treatises of every kind, that nothing can be less difficult than the arranging a plan for parish libraries. I look forward to a measure of this sort being without delay laid before the Government and if need be recommended to Parliament.

Report of the Parliamentary Committee on the State of Education (1834) 225.

Although the Society's publications were exempt from stamp duty, most pamphlets and newspapers were forced to carry duty which made them more expensive. A long campaign was fought to remove 'the taxes on knowledge', and many papers like the *Poor Man's Guardian* were established contrary to the law to try the power of 'Right against Might, Price 1d'.

During the 1830s many working men saw political activity as the only realistic way to improve their conditions. Among the Chartist leaders, men like William Lovett held strong convictions that only an educated and politically enlightened working class could bring changes in society. The publication of the People's Charter in 1838 had been preceded by the *Address on Education* in which Lovett declared his faith in popular education. In many towns Chartists opened reading rooms and hired halls for lectures and discussions. These ranged from Fine Art and Theology to Science and Political Economy. In many towns the educational activities of the Chartists were wide-ranging. They held day and Sunday schools, provided classes in reading and offered leisure-time activities like music and singing as well as the opportunity for political discussion. The Chartists' press constantly stressed the need for a reduction of the working day both for children and adults. Until they had more leisure, working people found it difficult to take full advantage of opportunities for self-improvement.

In many Chartist Halls and in Halls of Science opened by the disciples of Robert Owen, adults followed lectures which stressed utilitarianism, secularism and scientific study. A reaction against this teaching led to Anglicans and Nonconformists opening their own adult centres. Anglicans founded the Coventry Religious and Useful Knowledge Society, and in 1842 R. S. Bayley, a Congregationalist minister, founded a People's College in Sheffield. The College offered integrated studies with more concern than usual for the interest of the individual. F. D. Maurice, the Christian Socialist, and a group of friends founded the London Working Men's College on similar lines. Literate men over the age of sixteen could attend a wide range of classes including Bible classes. Maurice attracted as lecturers at the College Charles Kingsley, John Ruskin, Thomas Hughes and others who sympathized with his desire to provide a liberal rather than a utilitarian education.

The universities began to contribute to the teaching of adults through the inspiration of James Stuart, a lecturer at Cambridge. He had been educated in Scotland where university education was more widely available than in England. He considered arranging lecture tours for university professors and staff in large towns so that opportunities for higher education could be made more readily available. He envisaged a peripatetic university, and he described the beginning of his work, which became the University Extension Movement:

Saint David's College, Lampeter

I had no very clear notion of how the problem was to be tackled, but an obvious opportunity was given by a request, made to me in the early summer of 1867, to give lectures to ladies that autumn in Manchester, Liverpool, Sheffield and Leeds. There had been established, just at that time, in these four towns, an association calling itself the North of England Council for promoting the Higher Education of Women. Its president was Mrs Josephine Butler; its secretary was Miss A. J. Clough, and active members of it were Miss Wolstenholme in Manchester, Miss Theodosia Marshall and Miss Lucy Wilson in Leeds, and Dr and Mrs Keeting in Sheffield, as well as Mr Samuel Earnshaw (a clergyman in Sheffield, and a former Senior Wrangler) and a friend of his, Mr Samuel Roberts . . .

One day I was in some hurry to get away as soon as the lecture was over, and I asked the hall-keeper to allow my diagrams to remain hanging till my return next week. When I came back he said to me, 'It was one of the best things you ever did leaving up these diagrams. We had a meeting of our members last week, and a number of them who are attending your lectures, were discussing these diagrams, and they have a number of questions they want to ask you, and they are coming to-night a little before the lecture begins.' About twenty or thirty intelligent artisans met me about half an hour before the lecture began, and I found it so useful a half hour that during the remainder of the course I always had such a meeting.

W. H. Draper, *University Extension, 1873–1923* (1923) 9 and 14.

Stuart tried to win the support of the co-operative societies for his proposals to establish a peripatetic university. Their response was disappointing, and he turned to his own university of Cambridge for support. Stuart saw advantages for it to be associated with such a movement. He was convinced that the universities were beginning to face criticism for the narrowness of the social groups they served. He felt that by extending their activities such criticism could be forestalled. Cambridge appointed a syndic to examine the need. By 1873 the syndic undertook to organize courses of lectures supervised by the University in Nottingham, Derby and Leicester. The universities of London and Oxford began to provide similar lectures a few years later. A popular feature of the courses was the summer schools when, for a few weeks in the long vacation, the universities held residential courses connected with their extension lecture programmes. Some large towns provided colleges in which the lectures could take place, and many of these later developed into universities in their own right.

The university extension movement, like the mechanics' institutes, appealed particularly to men and women of the middle classes. The nature of the lectures and the fees charged seemed to have deterred working-class participation.

Another attempt at further education was made by Canon Samuel Barnett, Vicar of St Jude's Church, Whitechapel, when he established Toynbee Hall in 1885. This was to be a 'university settlement' containing lecture rooms and chambers for the accommodation of past and present university men: 'Some would come for the vacations; others occupied during the daytime would come to live there—university men, barristers, government clerks, curates, medical students or business men.' It established a pattern which was imitated by other settlements founded soon afterward. The essential idea was that those who had benefited from a university education should come to live among the poor and share with them what they had gained as undergraduates. An early resident gave an account of what he did there:

> As I was engaged all day reading in chambers, my leisure time was the evening. Before leaving Oxford I had engaged to take two reading parties at Toynbee Hall, one in Latin and another in English Literature . . . Soon some of the Latin class expressed a wish to learn Greek, so I added a third class. All three classes went on till well into the summer. Of the Latin and Greek class the majority were of the lower middle class—but one was a pupil teacher and one a foreman at the docks. In the Tennyson class I had a journeyman woodcarver, who also joined the 'Hume and Herbert Spencer' reading party which I formed somewhat later . . . It is still flourishing with a majority of the same members with whom it

> started and is at present in the throes of a final grapple with 'Transfigured Realism' and hopes soon to emerge into the humaner sphere of the ethical speculation.

Henrietta Barnett, *Canon Barnett* (1918) 1 vol ed, 327.

The early 1890s saw the classes at Toynbee Hall at the height of their popularity. From then their numbers began to decline until, by 1898, the number of students had fallen by a third. As the resident's account suggests, it was no more successful than the university extension movement in attracting many working-class students. Here also the membership of the classes and the subjects studied in them were attractive mainly to ambitious middle-class office workers and teachers.

A further effort to bring working-class people into contact with organized study was the establishment of residential colleges such as Woodbrooke and Fircroft. Three Americans, Mr and Mrs Vrooman and Professor Beard, founded Ruskin College, Oxford, where working men could be given 'a training in subjects which are essential for working-class leadership, and which are not a direct avenue to anything beyond'.

For those working men who desired a less politically oriented course, Albert Mansbridge founded the Workers' Education Association. He had attended the classes at Toynbee Hall and also university extension classes and those organized by the co-operative movement. As a London School Board teacher he met the adults who attended his evening classes in typewriting and history. He appreciated the weakness of the adult education that was available, and in 1898 he proposed a new approach. He hoped that the co-operative societies and the trade unions could work with the university extension movement to provide higher education of a liberal kind for working people. At Reading he found the local education authorities, the university and the local co-operative society ready to work together, and in 1903 the first WEA branch was founded. R. H. Tawney, the eminent historian, supported the venture and became one of the lecturers. He started the tutorial classes at Loughton and Rochdale, and these became a feature of the movement. Evening class work was supplemented by summer schools held in vacations at the universities. The Oxford Summer School was for many years the largest:

> The tutorial class system evolved during the fateful years 1907–10 constitutes a perfect expression of the partnership between learning and labour envisaged by Mansbridge since his earliest exciting encounter with the world of scholarship. Out from the universities went the tutors: young men and women at the outset of careers in university teaching and research or professors at the peak of academic

eminence; men and women to whom the salaries meant little but to whom the work meant much because it brought them into contact with a new range of students with a new range of interests and experiences and a new intensity of response. In Tawney's first Rochdale class was a young reporter from the local paper who in due course came to write the history of the cotton industry and edit the *Manchester Guardian* . . .

In the early tutorial classes men and women of exceptional natural ability, with no more than eight years or so of board-school teaching as an educational background, were learning the art of thought and the technique of free and fair discussion as well as the discipline of systematic study. Where the extension lecturer had provided a listening audience for an inspiring lecturer, the tutorial class, based as its name indicates on the tutorial methods of the ancient universities, provided an intimate intellectual contact between teacher and student in which the give and take of discussion was an essential feature. Hence the limitation of classes to a maximum of thirty enrolled students . . .

M. Stocks, *The Workers' Educational Association* (1953) 44–5, 60.

The movement spread rapidly, and within ten years there were 179 branches with 11,430 members, who were expected to read, take part in discussion and submit regular written work. Although the membership included manual workers and housewives, like the university extension movement and the mechanics' institutes, it had many middle-class students.

During the nineteenth century the role of adult education gradually changed. Many early adult schools concentrated on literacy for their members. The later adult schools had a literate membership and could provide courses of liberal and scientific studies to supplement the meagre education of so many men and women who left school at an early age.

5 Secondary education for the few

The French Revolution created an atmosphere of criticism of existing institutions, which, coupled with concern about state intervention, led some of the public schools and a few of the grammar schools to begin to reform themselves. Pressure from parents for a curriculum more relevant to an industrialized and commercial society started a process which continued throughout the nineteenth century.

The nine famous public schools—Winchester, Eton, St Paul's, Shrewsbury, Westminster, Merchant Taylors', Rugby, Harrow and Charterhouse—were the leading schools at the end of the eighteenth century. From them came about a third of the upper class in England. Their pupils went to the universities and in after life staffed the professions and government. From parents there was mounting criticism of the discipline, living conditions and conduct of the public schools.

Many contemporary writers justified the description of them as 'the very seats and nurseries of vice'. Edward Thring, later Headmaster of Uppingham, described life as he knew it at Eton in the 1830s:

> The old Long Chamber at Eton, now done away with for years, with its seventy boys locked up from 8 p.m. to next morning utterly without supervision, left entirely to themselves in the great, bare, dirty room in which they were supposed to live and did sleep. Who can ever forget that knew it the wild, rough, rollicking freedom, the frolic and the fun of that land of misrule, with its strange code of traditional boy-law, which really worked rather well as long as the sixth form were well disposed or sober? ... This wild college life was certainly a very different type from the sneak-as-you-please, but never-wet-your-feet existence of the private school, and it was the better of the two, for freedom is better than slavery; but alas! for the waste and ruin in the future, the wretchedness and coarseness and idleness at the time which it brought on the majority of those cast into its whirl.

G. R. Parkin, *Life of Edward Thring* (1910) 22.

R. Ackermann, 'Westminster School Room'

The effects of such an education on a boy were described by Dr Arnold, Headmaster of Rugby: 'Of all the painful things connected with my employment, nothing is equal to the grief of seeing a boy come to school innocent and promising and tracing the corruption of his character from the influence of temptations around him in the very place which ought to have strengthened and improved it.' (A. P. Stanley, *Life of Dr. Arnold* (1893) 65.)

Dr Butler described the problems he faced when he became Headmaster of Shrewsbury in 1798. He found schoolboys robbing the wine-cellars and getting dead drunk, boys stealing ducks by using baited lines and hooks. The local people complained that his boys terrorized them when they returned from holidays by riding on the tops of coaches and lashing passers by with whips and breaking windows with well-aimed volleys of stones.

This lawlessness inside and outside school hours reflected the violence of the age. It arose in the public schools because the numbers of staff and pupils were disproportionate. At Eton in 1834 there were only nine masters to control 570 boys. Order was maintained by contant floggings. Frequently the staff lost control, and open rebellion and riots broke out. Headmasters wrote letters to each other warning and seeking advice. The replies to a letter written by Samuel Butler of Shrewsbury in 1818 give an idea of the serious problems they faced. Dr Keate of Eton wrote to him:

> SIR,—I have received your letter of the 27th this morning, and am very sorry to perceive that the contagion of rebellion has reached your school also. I am sorry too to be thought to have sufficient experience to be referred to as an authority on these occasions. I beg leave, however, to assure you that I am very ready to give my opinion.
>
> The best answer I can return to your question, indeed the only one which I think I ought to give, is, that it has not been my practice either to rescind or to mitigate a sentence of expulsion. I was requested to do it upon one occasion some years ago, and I have been importuned in the same manner in six out of the seven late unfortunate instances, but I have uniformly resisted, thinking my public duty paramount to every consideration of private feeling.

And Dr Gabell of Winchester wrote:

> MY DEAR SIR,—You ask me if it is usual in cases of declared expulsion to change the sentence into dismission, or even revoke it altogether: I never heard of such a practice, nor do I recollect a single instance of it . . . No man could be more importuned than I was on a similar occasion, after our unfortunate distur-

bance last spring, but I thought it my duty to resist all importunity.

You have heard probably of the proceedings at Eton and at the Charterhouse, but perhaps you do not know that the Military College at Sandhurst has been in rebellion. The boys drew up in battle array against the professors.

S. Butler, *Life and Letters of Dr Samuel Butler* (1896) 2 vols, I, 158.

At both Winchester and Rugby the army were called into the schools to restore order. Sporadic outbreaks continued throughout the first half of the nineteenth century, the latest rebellion recorded being at Marlborough in 1851.

Within the schools criticism centred on the narrow curriculum. At Winchester Sidney Smith described with a shudder the horrors of his schooldays when he was forced to compose 10,000 Latin verses. He added, 'No man in his sense would dream in after life of making another. So much of life and time wasted.'

In the face of criticism and condemnation of their low moral tone, poor intellectual training and indiscipline, the schools might well have closed. Reform, however, came from within, mainly through the work of two great headmasters with the support of a number of parents who wanted to see the schools revitalized.

Samuel Butler was Headmaster of Shrewsbury School from 1798 to 1836. During his headship the school's ebbing fortunes revived, and it became a model for other public schools. Butler was an inspiring classicist who changed the antiquated methods of teaching. He encouraged hard work and good academic standards by examinations and promotion by merit. His pupils enjoyed considerable success in the Oxford and Cambridge scholarship examinations. Academic success depended upon good order in the school which Butler achieved partly through firmness towards trouble-makers. He encouraged responsibility among the older pupils by involving them in school government as praeposters. An appreciation of Butler's methods was expressed by the Master of St John's College, Cambridge, in 1818:

MY DEAR DR BUTLER,—Every member of the University interested in the support of discipline must feel thankful to you for the firmness with which you have resisted the turbulence and self-will of foolish and presumptuous boys. Children nowadays very early imbibe most pernicious notions, if not from their parents and relations, at least from the spirit of the times. I approve heartily of every point in your proceedings, and doubt not your school will stand as high in reputation for the due subordination and modesty of the scholars, as it does for their improvement in learning.

> I wish it may be consistent with your feelings either to give me the names of those whom you have advised to leave the school or to withhold the usual certificate of admission to St. John's. We have a very numerous, and, I am happy to say, a most respectable and orderly set of young men. I could not knowingly introduce any sowers of sedition among them. They have no rights here, but are under obligation to submit to the statutes, and such regulations as the Master and seniors may see necessary.
>
> *Ibid*, I, 163.

Butler saw his duty as a headmaster to train the character of all his boys, not merely to produce good scholars. He believed that boys should be self-reliant both in their studies, where he encouraged private reading, and in their personal conduct. The curriculum at Shrewsbury showed an enlightened approach. Pupils studied modern languages, modern history, mathematics and geography as well as the classics where the detailed study of grammar was modified. This curriculum was more in keeping with the changing needs of society. Butler followed the example of Thomas James, Headmaster of Rugby 1778–94, and made life more comfortable for the boys by giving them separate studies. Life in a public school became more humane, but much of the criticism of the schools in the early nineteenth century concerned moral tone. It was the influence of Thomas Arnold, Headmaster of Rugby 1828–42, that changed the public schools so that strict Churchmen and Nonconformists were anxious to send their boys to them. The attitude of Tom Brown's father expressed the attitude of many parents, 'If he'll only turn out a brave, helpful, truth-telling Englishman and a gentleman and a Christian, that's all I want.' Arnold's aim at Rugby was to create a Christian school, and he saw his position as a clergyman as vital to his success as a teacher. In the school chapel, Arnold exercised his personal influence to inspire his pupils with a sense of social duty as Christian gentlemen. He explained the unique position he felt the schoolmaster-clergyman enjoyed:

> The position of a schoolmaster in society has not yet obtained that respect in England as to be able to stand by itself in public opinion as a liberal profession. It owes the rank which it holds to its connection with the profession of a clergyman for that is acknowledged universally in England to be the profession of a gentleman. Mere teaching, like mere literature, places a man, I think, in a rather equivocal position. He holds no undoubted station in society by these alone for neither education nor literature have ever enjoyed that consideration and general respect in England which they enjoy in France and in Germany. But a far higher consideration is this, that he who is to educate boys, if he is full sensible of the

> importance of his business, must be unwilling to lose such great opportunities as the clerical character gives him to address them continually from the pulpit and to administer the Communion to them as they become old enough to receive it.
>
> T. Arnold, *Miscellaneous Works* (1845) 226.

It was particularly to the sixth form that Arnold looked for help in regenerating the moral tone of the school. He gave to the boys who became prefects considerable responsibility and authority:

> His zeal in its defence and his constant reliance upon it as the keystone of his whole government were eminently characteristic of himself. It was a point moreover on which the spirit of the age set strongly and increasingly against him, on which there was a general tendency to yield to the popular outcry, and on which the clamour, that at one time assailed him, was ready to fasten as a subject where all parties could concur in their condemnation. But he was immovable: and, though on his first coming he had felt himself called upon rather to restrain the authority of the Sixth Form from abuses, than to guard it from encroachments, yet now that the whole system was denounced as cruel and absurd, he delighted to stand forth as its champion. The powers, which was most strongly condemned, of personal chastisement vested in the Praeposters over those who resisted their authority, he firmly maintained as essential to the general support of the good order of the place; and there was no obloquy, which he would not undergo in the protection of a boy, who had by due exercise of this discipline made himself obnoxious to the school, the parents or the public.
>
> A. P. Stanley, *Thomas Arnold* (1893) 68.

While concerning himself with the moral tone of school, Arnold did not neglect the physical well-being of the pupils. He continued the work of his predecessor, Dr Wooll, in improving the accommodation in the school by providing separate studies and small, better supervised dormitories. Concern for improved academic standards led to a broadening of the curriculum to include subjects like French and mathematics which were no longer taken as extras by a few boys but widely studied. French and German, however, were taught as dead languages with no concern for pronunciation or reading of the texts. The teaching of classics underwent change. History became part of the curriculum. Demands made on staff and boys increased as the teachings became more efficient. In introducing these changes to Rugby, Arnold relied heavily on the young masters he appointed to his staff. He described the qualities he looked for when appointing a new master:

> . . . What I want is a man who is a Christian and a gentleman, an active man, and one who has common sense, and understands boys. I do not so much care about scholarship, as he will have immediately under him the lowest forms in the school; but yet, on second thoughts, I do care about it very much, because his pupils may be in the highest forms; and besides, I think that even the elements are best taught by a man who has a thorough knowledge of the matter. However, if one must give way, I prefer activity of mind and an interest in his work to high scholarship: for the one may be acquired far more easily than the other. I should wish it also to be understood, that the new master may be called upon to take boarders in his house, it being my intention for the future to require this of all masters as I see occasion, that so in time the boarding-houses may die a natural death . . . With this to offer, I think I have a right to look rather high for the man whom I fix upon, and it is my great object to get here a society of intelligent, gentlemanly, and active men, who may permanently keep up the character of the school, and make it 'vile damnum', if I were to break my neck to-morrow.
>
> *Ibid*, 61.

On some boys Arnold had very little effect so that the poet, Arthur Clough, could write, 'Even here at Rugby, the best of all public schools, which are the best kind of schools, even here there is a vast deal of bad.' Many of Arnold's young masters, inspired by his ideals, took them to other schools where they exercised a considerable influence. Harrow School was revived by one of Arnold's disciples. Many of Arnold's pupils went to Oxford and Cambridge where they brought a new climate of opinion reflecting the moral teaching which had been a vital part of their education. Later, many of his former pupils worked for social and political reforms.

Change came to the public schools, but it was often very slow, and old traditions died hard, as at Winchester:

> Our life at Winchester was certainly a narrow one in every way. We were shut off from the outside world. We were shut off from one another. We were shut off from the masters. Masters and boys lived in different worlds. I never spoke to a master except officially, on school business . . ., nor did it ever occur to me that there could be any other relation. The masters were simply another Creation.
>
> But the first real change in the relation began with the establishment of the first House in 1859. Still even then the Wykehamical tradition was so strong that I am assured that the first housemaster never went at night into his own boys' bedrooms without putting on his tall hat and overcoat.
>
> W. A. Fearon, *The Passing of Old Winchester* n.d. 20.

Nevertheless, the work of Butler and Arnold restored faith in public school education, and demand grew so that new schools were founded. The earliest was Cheltenham College in 1841, which was followed by Marlborough in 1842, Rossall in 1844, Wellington in 1859 and Clifton in 1860.

Cheltenham typified the new schools. It was financed by selling shares and, unlike a school supported by endowments, there were few restrictions imposed on the way it developed. Socially, however, it was so exclusive that the sons of tradesmen were not accepted:

> Had we admitted tradesmen in the first instance, we must have done so almost without limit, and in the confined circle of shops in Cheltenham, we should have had the sons of gentlemen shaking hands perhaps with schoolfellows behind the counter, and a fusion of ranks taking place from which the gentlemen of decided rank and prosperity would derive even less inconvenience possibly than the clergymen of confined income or half-pay officers.
>
> Letter of the Hon. Secretary of Cheltenham College. Quoted in T. W. Barnford 'The Rise of the Public Schools' (1967) 25.

The school served the sons of army and professional men and the curriculum expressed these interests. In the senior school, half the time was devoted to the classics and the rest to preparing candidates for the army and the civil service: Hindustani, Sanskrit and Persian could be studied as extras.

Wealthy businessmen sent their sons to such schools where they learnt the code of the gentry which meant that they rarely developed qualities leading to business success. The exclusive nature of many schools brought conflicts over the issue of endowments, particularly if the founder had made provision for the education of local boys. At Harrow in 1831 only fifteen of the 214 boys were on the foundation. The value of the emolument to these scholars was small. They were exempted from the fees of ten guineas for schooling (in classics) and one guinea for school charges. The foundationers paid fees for all other subjects and often for board and lodging; these could amount to a hundred guineas. As early as 1853 C. J. Vaughan, the Headmaster of Harrow, showed an awareness of the needs of local boys when he started a special form for them. Latin was taught freely in accordance with the will of the founder, but modern subjects were provided on payment of fees of £15 per annum. A similar pattern was followed at Oundle, where Laxton School was built.

While the public schools attracted growing support from the upper classes, many of the new industrial and commercial middle-class parents began to seek better standards of education for their children. Gladstone stressed this need when he opened Liverpool Collegiate School in 1843:

> There was this difference between the members of the middle and the members of the lower class. The members of the lower class in many instances exhibited a comparative indifference concerning the reception of education. To them the duty was not immediate and palpable. They pursued their daily purposes—but still education was not to them a necessity in order to enable them to labour with their hands; but when we looked at the middle classes—when we looked at those who were to carry on the commercial concerns of great towns—then we saw that an education there must be.
>
> *Illustrated London News*, 14th January 1843.

The great day schools, St Paul's, Merchant Taylors' and Manchester Grammar School, served the needs of the middle classes, while also meeting local demands. Samuel Bamford described his first impressions of Manchester Free Grammar School in 1800:

> The schoolroom was a large room of an oblong form, extending north and south and well-lighted by large windows. At the northern end was a fireplace with a red cheerful fire glowing in the grate. The master's custom was to sit in an armchair with his right side towards the fire and his left arm resting on a square oaken table, on which lay a newspaper or two, a magazine or other publication, a couple of canes with the ends split, and a medley of boys' playthings, such as tops, whips, marbles, applescraps, nutcrackers, dragon-binding and suchlike articles. The scholars were divided into six classes, namely accidence or introduction to Latin, higher Bible, middle Bible, lower Bible, Testament and spelling class; the accidence class sat opposite the master's face and the higher Bible one was at his back. Each class sat on a strong oaken bench backed by a panel of the same placed against the wall, with a narrow desk in front, so that all sat round the school in regular gradation. The spellers only had not a desk; they sat on forms outside the desk of the higher Bible class, they being considered as children among boys. The boys of each class were placed according to their proficiency, and the first and second boys of the class exercised considerable authority over the others. The school hours were from 7 to 8.30 at morning, from 9.30 to 12 at noon and from 2 till 5 in the afternoon.
>
> Samuel Bamford, *Passages in the Life of a Radical* (1893) I, 81–2.

At Manchester Free Grammar School teaching the classics was the main task, but where a grammar school only taught grammar it often failed to win local support. As early as 1795 Lord Chief Justice Kenyon, in giving judgment in a legal battle over the mastership of Skipton Grammar School, drew attention to the parlous state of many endowed grammar schools, a view amplified by Nicholas Carlisle, who made his own inquiry into the condition of the endowed schools in 1818:

> Whoever will examine the state of the grammar schools in the different parts of this kingdom will see to what lamentable condition most of them are reduced. I would wish that those who have any superintendence or control over them had been as circumspect as the Archbishop of York has been on the present occasion. If other persons had equally done their duty we should not find, as is now the case, empty walls without scholars and everything neglected but the receipt of salaries and emoluments.
>
> F. Vesey, *Chancery Reports*, II, 241.

> It is painful, however, to relate that many of our numerous local endowments have fallen to decay by the negligence or cupidity of ignorant or unprincipled trustees, who have silently or by connivance suffered the furtive alienation of the very lands which they were called upon so solemnly to defend, and which were in a great measure ordained for the education of their own children.
>
> As the property of those benevolent institutions is therefore in several cases lost or sunk; or embezzled or disgracefully misapplied, or lessened or impaired by gross dereliction of duty, and very great frauds committed in letting and managing the estates:- it appears absolutely necessary that such disorder and misapplication should speedily be abolished by a public investigation and a reform of those evils which is only within the power of Parliament.
>
> N. Carlisle, *The Endowed Grammar Schools of England and Wales* (1818) I, xxxv.

The state of the grammar schools revealed by Carlisle's inquiry and by the investigations of the Charity Commissioners between 1820 and 1840 showed great variations between the schools. Some with small endowments and ineffective governors had declined so seriously that buildings were dilapidated and scholars few. A number of former grammar schools had become National Schools, providing elementary instruction on monitorial lines. Other schools had adapted themselves successfully to the needs of the local population and were enjoying considerable prosperity. At Hexham and Burton-on-Trent the grammar schools offered instruction mathematics, navigation, English and history as well as the classics. A few old grammar schools in large commercial and industrial areas had a considerable reputation and attracted pupils from a distance. The grammar schools at Newcastle-upon-Tyne,

Bristol and Hull successfully combined modern subjects and a modern approach with classical teaching. The success of a school was often the work of an individual, as at Hull Grammar School where John Clarke, the Headmaster, wrote on education, published Latin texts and introduced new subjects into his school. Some grammar schools in rural areas were also well supported, as at Truro in Cornwall and North Walsham in Norfolk.

In contrast, change in the grammar school was hindered by the decision in a law suit brought before Lord Eldon, the Lord Chancellor, in 1806. At Leeds Grammar School, the governors, anxious to arrest the decline in the number of pupils, wanted the appointment of a master to teach writing, accounts and foreign languages to boys who attended to learn Latin and Greek. The headmaster and the usher of the school maintained that it was intended only for a grammar school, and a case was fought in Chancery. In giving his decision, Lord Eldon interpreted the intention of the founder as a desire to establish in Leeds 'a free grammar school for teaching grammatically the learned languages'. While Eldon was not averse himself to an extension of the curriculum, he was determined to uphold the intentions of the founders of many of the endowed schools and ensure that subjects specified in the foundation were taught. A school anxious to broaden the curriculum could do so provided it charged fees to cover the additional expenses. It was not until the Grammar Schools Act of 1840 that subjects other than those provided for in the foundation could be introduced.

For those who rejected the grammar school and the public school, there were a great variety of private schools. Parents were attracted to a school sometimes from religious convictions, sometimes by the curriculum. Some parents wanted their children to go away to boarding school, while some wanted the closer supervision of a private school. The quality of these schools varied considerably, and some were run by unprincipled owners with little knowledge of education, where living and educational standards were deplorably low. The advertisement in *The Times* for a school near Richmond in Yorkshire bears a strong resemblance to the advertisement for Dotheboys Hall in Dicken's novel, *Nicholas Nickleby*. The claims made for the schools were extravagant and the fees surprisingly low, and the parents who committed their children with few inquiries to these schools were as much to blame for the scandals that followed as the school speculators:

> Youths are boarded, Furnished with Books, and instructed in whatever their future prospects may require, for 20 and 22 guineas a year. No vacations unless desired. Cards, with references, to be had by return of post, and—will call upon applicants, after the 11th, in London.

> EDUCATION.—At Mr Wackford Squeers's Academy, Dotheboys Hall, at the delightful village of Dotheboys, near Greta Bridge in Yorkshire, Youth are boarded, clothed, booked, furnished with pocket-money, provided with all necessaries, instructed in all languages living and dead, mathematics, orthography, geometry, astronomy, trigonometry, the use of the globes, algebra, single stick (if required), writing, arithmetic, fortification, and every other branch of classical literature. Terms, twenty guineas per annum. No extras, no vacations, and diet unparalleled.

In contrast, some private schools promoted educational ideas and progressive attitudes. One of the earliest of these was Hazelwood School run by the Hill brothers at Birmingham. The school had a very liberal curriculum, an organization based on pupils' aptitudes and a novel method of control:

> The two great departments of education are government and instruction. We shall first speak of the government of our school. The principle on which we have acted has been to leave as much as possible all power in the hands of the boys themselves. To this end we permit them to elect a committee from their own body, in which the laws of the school are prepared, discussed and erected. The teachers having the regulation only of the routine of exercises, and the boys appointed for their performance; and these powers are not exercised individually, but by acts of the whole body, meeting in conference.
>
> *Plans for the Government and Liberal Instruction of Boys, in large numbers, as practised at Hazelwood School*, Anon, 1825.

To provide the kind of education they wanted for their children, parents subscribed to establish proprietary schools run as day schools on profit-making lines. In this way, day schools like the City of London School (1837) and University College School and King's College School (1829) were founded in London. A more ambitious venture was that of Nathaniel Woodard, who planned to establish a group of boarding schools of three grades for boys and girls in the Anglican tradition. Between 1832 and 1869 thirty-one schools were founded. Woodard explained his aims, making clear the groups in society he was trying to reach, in a letter to Bishop Fraser of Manchester in 1871:

> Somehow or other we must get possession of the Middle Classes, especially the lower section of them, and how can we so well do this as through Public Schools . . . Education without religion is in itself a pure evil—nothing more or less—and

Coloured lithograph by George Scharf, published in the 1830s. This shows the pupils of University College School in their playground with the buildings of University College in the background

> engenders the opposite form of selfishness to that which is the curse of an evil aristocracy ... Secular education makes Communists and Red Republicans ...
>
> J. Otter, *Nathaniel Woodward, A Memorial of His Life* (1925) 240–1.

Although school provision increased during the first half of the nineteenth century, many children were educated at home. Boys too young to go away to school had a tutor, while many girls had a governess. The schoolroom was a feature of the middle-class home:

> The schoolroom was high and narrow, with a very old carpet and a very old piano, some books, two globes and a good deal of feminine rubbish in the way of old work-baskets, unfinished sewing, etc. There were two long windows, the lower halves of which were covered with paint. This mattered the less as the only view from them was of backyards, roofs and chimneys.
>
> J. H. Ewing, *A Flat-Iron for a Farthing* (1873).

The governesses taught their charges reading and writing, sometimes a little history and French and usually accomplishments like music, needlework and painting. Themselves ill-educated, they had little knowledge and few interests to pass on to the girls. Without qualifications they could command only low wages for which they worked long hours in lonely isolation, often far from family and friends. Charlotte Brontë, who did much to make her readers aware of the unenviable lot of governesses, described her own experiences in a letter to her sister, Emily, in 1839:

> I have striven hard to be pleased with my new situation [as governess at Mr John Sidgewick's house at Stonegappe]. The country, the house and the grounds are, as I have said, divine; but, alack-a-day, there is such a thing as seeing all beautiful around you, pleasant woods, white paths, green lawns and blue sunshiny sky—and not having a free moment or a free thought left to enjoy them. The children are constantly with me. As for correcting them, I quickly found that was out of the question; they are to do as they like. A complaint to the mother only brings black looks on myself and unjust partial excuses to screen the children ... I said in my last letter that Mrs Sidgwick did not know me. I now begin to find she does not intend to know me; that she cares nothing about me except to contrive how the greatest possible quantity of labour may be got out of me, and to that end she overwhelms me with oceans of needlework; yards of cambric to hem, muslin nightcaps to make and, above all things, dolls to dress ... I see more clearly than I have ever done before that a private governess has no existence, is not con-

sidered as a living, rational being, except as connected with the wearisome duties she has to fulfill.

Quoted in Mrs Gaskell, *Life of Charlotte Bronte* (1900) 173.

Sympathy for the plight of the governesses led to the founding of the Governesses' Benevolent Institution in 1841. F. D. Maurice, a leading Christian Socialist, determined to improve the educational qualifications of governesses, planned a series of lectures, and from these beginnings developed Queen's College, Harley Street, where middle-class women and girls could gain a sound education. Among the first pupils were Frances Mary Buss, later the founder and Headmistress of the North London Collegiate School for Girls, and Dorothea Beale, later Principal of the Ladies College at Cheltenham. With other enlightened women, they changed the nature of girls' education in their schools and provided a curriculum similar to that of the boys' schools.

Educational provision for the upper and middle classes increased in the first half of the nineteenth century, but concern for quality grew rapidly and was voiced by Matthew Arnold:

> ENGLISH secondary instruction wants, I said, two things: sufficient provision of good schools, sufficient security for these schools continuing good. Granting that the Universities may give us the second, I do not see how they are to give us the first. It is not enough merely to provide a staff of inspectors and examiners, and still to leave the children of our middle class scattered about through the numberless obscure endowed school and 'educational homes' of this country. . . . What is wanted for the English middle class is *respected* schools as well as *inspected* schools.

Leonard Huxley (ed), *Thoughts on Education from Matthew Arnold* (1912), 99–100.

6 The development of the universities

> A traveller who visits Oxford or Cambridge is surprised and edified by the apparent order and tranquillity that prevails in the seats of the English muses . . . The use of arms is banished from our English universities; the uniform habit of the academics, the square cap and black gown, is adapted to the civil and even clerical professions; and from the doctor in divinity to the undergraduate, the degrees of learning and age are externally distinguished . . . The students of Oxford and Cambridge are united in colleges; the maintenance is provided at their own expense or that of the founders; and the stated hours of the hall and chapel represent the discipline of a regular and as it were religious community.
>
> Edward Gibbon, *Autobiography* (1950) Oxford World's Classics, 34.

At the beginning of the nineteenth century Oxford and Cambridge had a monopoly of higher education in England. They faced criticism of their exclusiveness and the irrelevance of the education they provided. Dissenters were prevented from entering Oxford or taking a degree at either university by the obligation to subscribe to the Thirty-Nine Articles. In 1789 Vicesimus Knox was urging that 'all useless and antiquated forms whatever, which savour of monkery, popery, slavery and Gothicism, should be utterly abolished'. He was referring particularly to the oaths taken at Oxford. It was not until 1827 that the oath not to attend or give lectures at Stamford was abolished, and Dissenters were only freed from their disadvantages late in the nineteenth century. The Church of England feared these attacks on its monopoly and resisted change.

The universities were also attacked for their narrow curriculum and inefficient examining systems. Sydney Smith in the *Edinburgh Review* in 1810 condemned them for being out of touch with the needs of the time in their outlook:

> A learned man! a scholar! a man of erudition! Upon whom are these epithets of approbation bestowed? Are they given to men acquainted with the science of government? thoroughly masters of the geographical and commercial relations

of Europe? to men who know the properties of bodies and their action upon each other? No; this is not learning; it is chemistry, or political economy—not learning. The distinguishing abstract term, the epithet of scholar, is reserved for him who writes on the Aeolic reduplication and is familiar with Sylburgius his method of arranging defectives in ω and μι ... His object is not to reason, to imagine, or to invent; but to conjugate, decline and derive ... Would he ever dream that such men as Adam Smith and Lavoisier were equal in dignity or understanding to, or of the same utility as, Bentley and Heyne?

Quoted in V. H. H. Green, *The Universities* (1969) 50.

In reply to this view that the older universities made little contribution to the intellectual movements of the time, Edward Copleston, an influential don, defended the liberality of Oxford education: 'Never let us believe that the improvement of chemical arts, however much it may tend to the augmentation of the national riches, can supersede the use of that intellectual laboratory where the sages of Greece explored the hidden elements of which man consists and faithfully recorded all their discoveries.' (E. Copleston, *Reply to Calumnies* (1810) 133–4.)

Although the university curriculum was dominated by the classics at the beginning of the nineteenth century scientific studies had found a place. These were usually introduced by enthusiastic individuals and often limited to the provision of a course of lectures. At Cambridge in 1794 a series of lectures on applied science was given by the Professor of Chemistry, W. Farrish of Magdalene College:

The application of chemistry to the arts and manufactures of Britain prescribed a new and useful field of instruction, which, however, could not be cultivated with effect without exhibiting whatever else was necessary to the full illustration of the subject. After having taken an actual survey of curios in the manufactures of the Kingdom, the Professor contrived a mode of exhibiting operations and processes that are in use in nearly all of them. Having provided himself with a number of brass wheels of all forms and sizes ..., he constructs ... working models of almost every kind of machine.

C. Wordsworth, *Scholae Academicae* (1910) 345.

By 1800 Cambridge had chairs in geology, botany and astronomy, while at Oxford there were lectures in experimental philosophy, natural philosophy, astronomy and chemistry, so that both universities were training some scientists, although the initiative for advancing a subject rested with the individual professor or head of a college.

In Oxford the first moves came to reorganize the examination system. John Napleton, a tutor at Brasenose College, published anonymously in 1773 *Considerations of the Public Exercises for First and Second Degrees*. He described the oral disputations as 'lifeless, unedifying formalities', and he condemned the lack of supervision of the examinations as well as their low standards. Vicesimus Knox added his support, describing in detail the empty farce of an examination where 'the greatest dunce could get a degree along with the greatest genius'. John Eveleigh, Provost of Oriel, Cyril Jackson, Dean of Christ Church, and John Parsons, Master of Balliol, led a reform group which successfully passed new Examination Statutes through Congregation in 1800. This introduced formidable examinations for Honours degrees. Separate schools for mathematics, physics and literae humaniores developed. Later the Pass and Honours degrees were separated, and a system of classes was introduced. As the number of candidates increased, written examinations were introduced. Similar changes took place at Cambridge where a modern examination system centring upon new triposes stimulated intellectual life. By the 1820s the examinations themselves were being criticized for their narrowing effect on studies. The inadequacies of lecturing and tutoring at the universities were also revealed, and many students found themselves forced to study with private tutors in order to pass the examinations—a practice they found expensive.

Criticism of the collegiate system grew throughout the century. In many colleges, the fellows lived a retired life, little troubled by the demands of students or scholarship, and were anxious to avoid change which might disturb their comfort. When Mark Pattison was appointed to a fellowship at Lincoln College in 1839, he described four of the fellows as 'fossil specimens' and expressed the view that Lincoln, Queen's, Magdalen, Jesus and St John's had fallen low in prestige among the colleges. In contrast, the reformers, Parsons and Eveleigh, threw the fellowships of their colleges at Balliol and Oriel to open competition and drew some talented men to Oxford.

Progress might have been greater had religious controversy not absorbed energy which could have been directed towards reform. At Cambridge the Evangelical movement led by Charles Simeon, Vicar of Holy Trinity Church, Cambridge, greatly affected college life. Later at Oxford the Tractarian movement centred upon John Keble and John Henry Newman, who began to issue their *Tracts for the Times*, and bitter controversy followed which led eventually to the resignation of Newman. Mark Pattison expressed his relief at the departure of the Tractarians 'as deliverance from the nightmare which had oppressed Oxford for fifteen years'. The religious dissension at Oxford and Cambridge diverted attention from scholarship and from the need to reassess the function of the universities in the changing society of the times.

This religious activity was taking place at the same time as discussion in the House of Commons of a bill to admit Dissenters to the universities. Churchmen were determined that no change should take place in the character of the universities, and the bill was defeated. The critics of the universities, led by men like Sir William Hamilton, looked to the State to carry out the reforms which so many felt were necessary. In 1850 Lord John Russell appointed a Royal Commission to inquire into the State, Discipline, Studies and Revenues of Oxford and Cambridge.

Some years earlier a Royal Commission of 1826 had examined the Scottish universities—St Andrew's, Edinburgh and Glasgow. Although no government action followed the report, a number of reforms were initiated by the universities themselves. A similar outcome was expected by many who cared for the future of the older universities. There were some, however, who were strongly opposed to a commission. A writer in the *Quarterly Review* urged action to protect the universities; he reminded his readers that:

> Nothing can compel the colleges against their will to be parties to any such usurped interference, but to punish the colleges for refusing to be visited; that is, for refusing to violate their oaths and to submit to what is neither more nor less than a gross act of democratical tyranny; and if the day is now at hand when the liberties and consciences of Englishmen are to be trampled on by the evil power which they themselves have created in a usurping House of Commons, this, we trust, will be the course adopted. Let the ministry or the legislature be dared to such an aggression upon the colleges. Let them be compelled, if their end is to be gained, to gain it by an act of oppression, overturning all the principles of our laws and the safeguards of our constitutional rights. Let the members of those colleges avow their willingness to be ejected from their homes and their livelihoods, rather than by an act of cowardice and compromise to aid and abet this newly-established tyranny, in violation of their oaths to their founders and of their allegiance to the Church. They are indeed obedient to the legislature of their country. No one for one moment would urge them to resist its laws; but obedience has always an alternative. Let them submit to the penalty, not to be parties to the act, and if any one thing can open the eyes of the people and lay bare the real character of its democracy, it will be such a persecution of the universities of this country as was planned in Lord Radnor's last bill . . . No Whig ministry will have the courage and the principles to attack a body which

threatens them with resistance. It is not in their nature: give way and they immediately oppress; but meet them face to face, and they are quiet and submissive in an instant. They have neither will nor opinion of their own and profess to be guided only by the pressure of others. Let the Universities stand firm. They may defy all external aggression as their founders intended them to defy it.

Quarterly Review (1837) 59.

Whatever might be the outcome of the Royal Commission's inquiry, many parents felt an education at the older universities was unacceptable for their children. Too often they were less concerned with the irrelevant curriculum or the religious strife than with the expense of a university education. In 1852 the Commissioners commented upon this problem: 'On the whole, we believe that a parent, who, after supplying his son with clothes and supporting him at home during the vacations, has paid for him during his university course not more than £600 and is not called upon to discharge debts at its close, has reason to congratulate himself.' (*Report of the Royal Commission on Oxford* (1852) 33.) For these parents, usually members of the middle class, an alternative form of higher education seemed desirable. Looking at the example of the United States of America and Germany, they found much to admire in the character of new university institutions. It was after a visit to Germany in 1820 that Thomas Campbell, Editor of the *New Monthly Magazine*, eventually proposed a new kind of university institution. He wrote in a letter addressed to Henry Brougham:

The plan which I suggest is a great London University, not a place for lecturing to people of both sexes (except as an appendage to the establishment) but of effectively and multifariously teaching, examining, exercising and rewarding with honours in the liberal arts and sciences, the youth of our middling rich people, between the age of 15 or 16 and 20.

The Times, 9th February 1825.

From this initiative a meeting was held, committees were formed, and among the leaders were Henry Brougham, George Birkbeck, and Jeremy Bentham and James Mill. A joint-stock company was created, and the council said:

When it is considered, therefore, how great must be the number and opulence of those who do not belong to the Established Church, and how large a portion of the people of England consists of persons in easy yet moderate circumstances, there cannot be a doubt that the best interests of the country urgently demand the establishment of an institution where an enlightened education may be obtained at a reasonable charge and where persons of every religious persuasion may be freely admitted.

Statement of the Council of the University of London, quoted in D. K. Douglas (ed), *English Historical Documents 1783–1832* (1959) 697.

In October 1828 in Gower Street, Bloomsbury, London University received its first students 'to study various branches of knowledge which are objects of a liberal education'. Its founders were influenced by the example of Edinburgh University rather than Oxford or Cambridge. It admitted its students without religious tests and gave no place to theology in its curriculum. Those who valued the religious element in education rallied their forces even before London University opened its doors, and at a public meeting presided over by the Duke of Wellington in June 1828 resolved:

That it is the opinion of this meeting that a college for general education be founded in the metropolis in which, while the various branches of literature and science are made the subjects of instruction, it shall be an essential part of the system to imbue the minds of youth with a knowledge of the doctrines and duties of Christianity as inculcated by the United Church of England and Ireland.

F. J. C. Hearnshaw, *Centenary History of King's College* (1928) 41.

King George IV agreed to become the patron of the new foundation in the Strand, which opened in October 1831.

Commenting on the opening of the two colleges, Lord Grey wrote to Henry Brougham:

It must afford the truest satisfaction to everybody who thinks, as I do, of the public benefit likely to arise from such an institution. But to you it must be peculiarly gratifying, for you have been the creator of this establishment, and your name will be for ever united with the improvements which may spring, not only from this, but from the rival college which never would have existed but for the success of your exertions.

H. Brougham, *Autobiography* (1871), 3 vols, III, 500.

The new university was bitterly opposed by Oxford and Cambridge, and it was not until 1836 that London University was empowered to grant degrees. At this time the University in Gower Street was renamed University College. London University became a purely examining body, prepared to examine anybody who matriculated.

This made possible the development of external degrees, and the number of candidates gaining qualifications in this way grew steadily.

In the North, the Dean and Chapter of Durham Cathedral founded a university, partly to meet the need for higher education in the North, but also to ward off Radical attacks on Cathedral revenues. Prebendary Durrell wrote in 1831:

> As soon as the Reform Bill is disposed of, an attack will be made on deans and chapters, and it is certain that Durham will be the first object. It has occurred to us that it will be prudent if possible to ward off the blow, and that no plan is so likely to take as making the public partakers of our income by annexing an establishment of enlarged education to our college.
>
> V. H. H. Green, *op cit*, 108.

The progressive group at Durham ensured that the curriculum was wide and included courses in engineering as well as science, arts and theology. The new university adopted the collegiate system of Oxford rather than the non-residential pattern of London.

Other foundations followed—one of the earliest was Owens College, at Manchester, in 1851. The generosity of John Owens, a wealthy Nonconformist, made possible the provision of a college to serve the business and commercial interests of the city. The University Colleges at Birmingham and Sheffield (1880) also owed much to local individual generosity, and the University of Wales was the outcome of local national feeling. The new foundations showed a growing awareness of the social functions of a university education.

The early hopes of these new universities were only slowly fulfilled. Within a few years they faced falling enrolments of students and grave financial difficulties. The system of secondary education in England in the middle of the nineteenth century was inadequate for the preparation of large numbers of pupils for higher education. Perhaps because of the expense of a university course, fewer people seemed anxious to avail themselves of university education than was anticipated. University staffs were poorly paid, and it became difficult to attract able men. Nevertheless the colleges persisted, and many achieved much, acting as a stimulus for the older universities in the process.

While the provincial universities were developing a new style of university life, the Royal Commission on Oxford and Cambridge carried out its inquiry and made a report. The Commissioners stressed the limitations of the curriculum, the expense of undergraduate life and the inadequacies of the university government:

It has been held to be the sole business of the University to train the powers of the mind, not to give much positive or any professional knowledge; and the study of the classical books is regarded as the best means of refining and invigorating the mind. The education given has hitherto been the same for all, whether clergymen or barristers, medical men or private gentlemen. It has been limited to such subjects as were presumed to be common to all these kinds of life; and no one has left Oxford, under the system hitherto pursued, much more fitted for one profession than another.

A different theory of education prevailed . . . when the ancient statutes were drawn up. In those days youths usually came to the university at a very early age and stayed many years. At first they found it a mere grammar school, but afterwards a place where all the knowledge of the age might be deeply studied. At the present day, young men come into residence at a much more advanced age, and yet the university is for the majority of them a mere grammar school from first to last. We have no desire that professional education in the strict sense of the word should be given in Oxford. But the University has long been moving into the opposite extreme, and it has been a serious loss both to Oxford and the learned professions that the studies which would prepare young men to enter a professional life should have been so completely neglected . . .

There is much in medical and legal studies which cannot be effectually taught at the University; so also of Engineering, Agriculture, Politics, etc. But there is not one of these professions for which the University will not very effectually educate in the most essential and fundamental particulars if she do but heartily and faithfully carry out the system which she has recently established. As society is constituted for the present I see no necessity for more than this. It is one of the peculiarities of our social condition that we have too much rather than too little time to learn the specialities of the higher branches of professions; and it has hitherto been the evil of our system of education, that a good foundation in general knowledge has not been laid through which those specialities can be approached effectively and in a liberal spirit . . .

Of the changes required, perhaps the most important is that of removing restrictions on the elections to Fellowships. The most injurious are those which confine the Fellowships to natives of particular localities, to members of particular families and to those who are or have been Scholars in the College. The result of these various limitations, whether imposed by Statute or the practice of Colleges, is that of 540 Fellowships there are scarcely 20 which are open to general competition; and of these, few, if any, can be considered as absolutely free from statutable restrictions.

Every other recommendation we propose depends in a greater or lesser degree on the removal of these restrictions . . . The system of election to Fellowships is above all other defects at Oxford that whose remedy is most needed and most important. The Fellows are so completely the governing body of the University that if no other change were made, to throw all the fellowships open and secure that the elections were honest, all other reforms would follow spontaneously. A body of men elected in the interests of learning would be sure in course of time to adapt everything to the needs of learning.

We will show the evils arising from the system of close fellowships . . . Men who are naturally well-fitted to become country clergymen are bribed, because they were born in some parish in Rutland, to remain in Oxford as Fellows until they are not only unfit for that, but for everything else. The interests of learning are entrusted to those who have neither talents nor inclination for the subject. The Fellowships are looked upon and used as mere stepping-stones to a living. A large number of the Fellows live away from the place and thus in reality convert the emoluments to a purpose quite alien from that for which they were intended. On the other hand, the undergraduates suffer a double loss, first in being deprived of the legitimate stimulus to study, and secondly, in having their instruction entrusted to an inferior body of men.

Report of the Royal Commission on Oxford (1852) 149–51.

The Commissioners recommended the development of new Honour schools for science and mathematics and the revival of the schools of law and medicine. To meet the needs, the colleges were urged to appoint additional professors. Concern at the expense of undergraduate life and criticism of the abuses of closed scholarships and fellowships showed the Commissioners' desire to see a wider social group at the older universities. They deplored that 'there is one large class of the community which is excluded not through poverty . . . namely, those who are unwilling to subscribe to the Thirty-Nine Articles of the Church of England'.

Some of the recommendations of the Commissioners were made effective by the University Reform Bills of 1854 (Oxford) and 1856 (Cambridge). These removed religious tests for students wishing to matriculate and take a first degree. The colleges gained time to revise their own statutes, and new attitudes to teaching and research followed the appointment of liberal academics like Mark Pattison, Rector of Lincoln, and Benjamin Jowett, Master of Balliol. According to Pattison, the 1850s saw 'more improvement in the tempo and teaching of Oxford than the three centuries which went before'. In 1871 all religious tests were abolished.

This change at the universities enabled them to extend their influence in other ways. One vexed educational question concerned the growth of examinations, and there was support for the view of Frederick Temple (later Archbishop of Canterbury) expressed in a letter to Robert Scott, Master of Balliol, in 1857:

> Similar ideas are afloat everywhere, and it would require but a slight impulse to make the system general. The government will not take this in hand, the Society of Arts is well enough as a leader of Mechanics' Institutes, but has neither the prestige nor the organization to be more.
>
> Will there be any change of inducing the Universities to step in? My plea is this—
>
> That the University should appoint a competent Board of Examiners; that the examiners should be prepared to examine all boys between certain ages presented to them under certain regulations; that the examination should be divided into schools to cover the subjects at present most needed by boys in the middle class schools . . .; that the expenses of the examination should be covered by a small fee for the candidate.
>
> W. R. Ward, *Victorian Oxford* (1965) 281.

By 1870 Oxford and Cambridge were setting examinations which were taken by both boys and girls in the grammar and public schools. The universities thus began to determine school curriculum standards. Reform at the universities continued when a further Commission of 1872 examined their revenues, and legislation led to the establishment of new chairs and readerships. Enlivened intellectual activity led to pressure for more reform:

> The further reforms which are called for originate in the intellectual activity of the universities themselves, even more than in that spirit of the age which is supposed to be always seeking to criticize and remodel. A restless intellectual fervour has taken possession of the most able residents, and propagandist spirit has been developed which desires to carry university teaching and university influence to every corner of the land.
>
> *The Times*, 21st August 1873.

The transformation of the older universities and the growth of the new universities provoked discussion on the role and purpose of the universities in society. As early in 1809 a writer in the *Edinburgh Review* had asked, 'What other measure is there of dignity in intellectual labour but usefulness? And what ought the term university to mean but a place where every science is taught which is liberal and at the same time useful to mankind?' (*Edinburgh Review*, 29th October 1809.)

T. H. Huxley, an ardent protagonist for science, expressed the same view:

> At present the universities make literature and grammar the basis of education, and they actually pride themselves upon their liberality when they stick a few bits of science on the outside of the fabric. Now that, in my apprehension, is not real culture, nor is it what I understand by a liberal education. The thing you really have to do is, in my opinion, to invert the whole edifice and to make the foundation science, and literature the superstructure and final covering.
>
> *Select Committee on Scientific Instruction* (1868).

Huxley touched the core of a problem which was particularly relevant in the later years of the nineteenth century when university expansion was taking place. The new provincial universities had much in common—they were democratic and secular—they accepted women students equally with men—most were non-residential, and lecturing was the usual mode of instruction. Often they offered a specialized and limited curriculum and their students, usually drawn from the lower middle class, lacked the cultural background and traditions of those who had gone to universities in the past.

Did the education gained at London University or a provincial university 'make a better man'? This question was asked by Victorians, who looked to the older universities, as they did to the public schools, to train character and produce leaders. For Jowett, the function of a university was the education of its students for life rather than the furthering of scholarship through research. This accorded with the views expressed by J. H. Newman when he lectured at Dublin in 1852 and put forward his 'Idea of a University'. Newman looked to the university to provide a wide range of studies which would be liberal not utilitarian. In this way students would become well-educated men capable of thinking and reasoning.

Ten years later Mark Pattison in *Suggestions on Academical Organisation* urged the universities to engage in research, and he looked for more specialization. He felt strongly that the education of the undergraduate was only one purpose of the university, and he urged the pursuit of excellence. While these ideas were under discussion, English universities were influenced by the developments in Germany. Jowett described, 'The German ocean lapping round the walls of every university in Britain—new and old alike.' The number of research students at British universities increased, reflecting the German universities' stress on post-graduate studies.

Another development which brought change to the universities was the admission of women in the latter part of the nineteenth century. This was achieved only after a long struggle inspired and conducted by Emily Davies and a small group of supporters. The first stage in the struggle came in 1862 with the rejection of Elizabeth Garrett's application to sit the examinations for matriculation of London University so that she could train as a doctor. This drew attention to the injustices facing women seeking higher education. After considerable pressure from the protagonists, Cambridge University allowed girls to sit its Local Examinations in 1865 as an experiment, and two years later the examination scheme for girls became a permanent one. Meanwhile, Emily Davies became convinced that a new college must be founded to meet the needs of women in higher education. Her opponents asked, 'Does anyone in his (or her) senses suppose that the understanding of average young ladies would be the better for passing this examination [the London B.A. degree] well, or for trying to pass it anyhow, as the proper aim of their education? . . . I believe that we should have half the young women in the country in brain fever or a lunatic asylum, if they were to make up their minds to try for it.' (Quoted in Josephine Kamm, *Hope Deferred* (1965) 250.)

At Cambridge, Emily Davies had more enlightened friends, and after many difficulties a college at Hitchin, linked with the University, was opened, and the students began to read for the University Tripos in 1869. Five years later the College was incorporated as Girton College and moved to Cambridge. A year later Anne Clough opened another college for women at Newnham. Although women students were taking and passing the Tripos examinations, they were not awarded degrees, despite the high achievements of a Girton student, Agnata Ramsay, the only candidate placed in the first division of the first class of the Classical Tripos in 1887, and Philippa Fawcett, a Newnham student, who was placed above the Senior Wrangler. Cambridge did not admit women to the title of degrees until 1921.

At Oxford, Lady Margaret Hall and Somerville College were established for women, and London University in 1878 and the Victoria University at Manchester in 1850 opened their degrees to women. By this time women were being freely admitted to the centres of higher education.

The advance in university education for women was but part of the steady expansion which had taken place at both the older and the newer universities by the early twentieth century. At the same time the English university system had retained a unique character which William Temple expressed in his Presidential Address to the Workers Educational Association in 1915:

When . . . I praise the English traditional education, I am praising education by means of a corporate life . . . Our intellectual training has often been very amateurish in method and very feeble in result. We most undoubtedly need strengthening here. But you will observe at once that it just here, and here alone, that German education has been strong; it has not aimed at the sub-conscious mind, as ours has done—moulding the whole personality by the silent appeal to imagination and sympathy which a common tradition embodied in a social life is alone able to make. That is the only way to train those elements in our nature which determine how we shall act in an emergency, when there is no time for reflection, or when ordinary standards are displaced . . .

F. A. Iremonger, *William Temple* (1948) 60.

7 The period of the commissions

With the creation of the Committee of the Council, the government asserted civil as opposed to ecclesiastical authority in education. At first the Committee was controlling the distribution of grants, but it also claimed the right of inspection as a condition of their receipt. The National Society opposed inspection and at first refused grants rather than accept the principle. In July 1840 a Concordat was negotiated between the Church and the government which made important concessions:

> That before we recommend to your Majesty any person to be appointed to inspect Schools receiving aid from the public, the promoters of which state themselves to be in connexion with the National Society or the Church of England, we should be authorized to consult the Archbishops of Canterbury and York, each with regard to his own province, and that the Archbishops should be at liberty to suggest to us any person or persons for the office of Inspector, and that without their concurrence we should recommend no person to your Majesty for such appointment.
>
> We further beg leave to recommend to your Majesty that if either of the Archbishops should at any time, with regard to his own province, withdraw his concurrence in our recommendation of such appointment, your Majesty would be graciously pleased to permit us to advise your Majesty to issue an Order in Council, revoking the appointment of the said Inspector, and making an appointment in lieu thereof . . .
>
> *Order in Council Dated August 10th 1840, Recording the Concordat with the Archbishop of Canterbury Concerning the Inspection of Schools.*

Similar agreements were reached with the Roman Catholics and the other denominations. In 1840 the first two inspectors were appointed, and Kay-Shuttleworth gave them instructions which set out the aims of inspection:

> . . . 3. In superintending the application of the Parliamentary grant for public education in Great Britain, my Lords have in view the encouragement of local

efforts for the improvement and extension of elementary education, whether made by voluntary associations or by private individuals. The employment of Inspectors is therefore intended to advance this object, by affording to the promoters of schools an opportunity of ascertaining, at the periodical visits of inspection, what improvements in apparatus and internal arrangements of schools, in school management and discipline, and in the methods of teaching, have been sanctioned by the most extensive experience . . .

Minutes of the Committee of Council (1840–1) 1–2.

The reports of the inspectors gave a wealth of information to the Council so that educational needs could be appreciated. The government was beginning to concern itself with quality and standards in education. The Secretary gave the inspectors long schedules of questions to complete, and from the reports something can be learnt of the way the classes were taught:

At Stockton, St Thomas Infants School, 105 children attended on average. Buildings, a fair-sized room, with a large gallery, two rooms for mistress above the school-room. Playground, good-sized playground. Furniture, clock, stove. Books and apparatus, one slate, three reading stands, one abacus. Discipline very fair. Sewing and knitting, none. No registers kept of daily attendance. Organization, the majority of lessons given to the whole school in the gallery; four classes for the alphabet, three classes for reading.

D. J. Stewart, *Tabulated Reports of Schools Inspected in Counties of Northumberland, Durham, Cumberland and Westmoreland* (1855).

With the development of the pupil-teacher scheme by Kay-Shuttleworth, the inspectors became involved in teacher training, approving teachers who might take apprentices and examining the pupil-teachers. Through the teachers the inspectors hoped to spread new ideas and foster improvements.

Plans to extend educational provision through Parliamentary legislation foundered on the denominational issue until 1870. The first attempt was made by Sir James Graham when he introduced educational clauses into a Factory Bill. A strong, dissenting agitation against the scheme led to its withdrawal. Sir Robert Peel, the Prime Minister, explained the problem to the Queen in a letter, which revealed the strength of religious feeling in 1843:

In consequence of the persevering and general opposition of the Dissenting Body to the proposed measure of the Government for providing combined scriptural education for the children employed in factories, and the little prospect that they would, even if the Bill were carried, unite in giving effect to it, your Majesty's servants thought it better to withdraw the measure than make an attempt to carry it, which, as success depended upon general concord and goodwill, must be ultimately unavailing, and the progress of which must infallibly embitter religious animosity and strife.

C. S. Parker, *Sir Robert Peel* (1899) ii 561.

Despite this failure, Parliamentary support to voluntary schools continued to rise so that by 1856 it amounted to £541,233 a year. The creation of the Education Department in that year and the appointment of a Vice-President of the Council, who was a member of the government and responsible to Parliament, showed the determination to control more closely educational expenditure. Outside Parliament, societies to further particular educational interests developed. For many people frustrated by religious disputes, the Lancaster Public School Association, with its proposals for secular schools, seemed to offer progress. The Voluntaryists formed a strong group to support their view that religion was the first element in education.

Sir John Packington, a Conservative Member of Parliament keenly interested in education, having failed to get two bills through Parliament, proposed a Commission to survey the state of popular education as a preliminary to further legislation to extend to all classes of people 'sound and cheap elementary instruction'. The Commission began its work in 1858. When it reported in 1861, it concluded that of 2,655,767 of the poorest classes of school age, 2,535,767 were in schools. The Commissioners found that many pupils failed to learn even to read and write through frequent absence and early leaving. This was understandable, 'When it is remembered that agricultural wages range from 9s to 14s or 16s a week and that children can add to this sum sometimes as much as 4s or 5s and generally 2s 6d, the importance of their earnings to their parents becomes sufficiently apparent.' (*Newcastle Report* (1861) VII, 1, 182.)

The recommendations of the Commissioners included simplification of the way grants were paid to the schools and supplementation by payment from the rates. To ensure more effective use of resources they suggested:

There is only one way of securing this result which is to institute a searching examination by competent authority of every child in every school to which grants are paid with a view to ascertaining whether these indispensable elements of knowledge are thoroughly acquired and to make the prospects and positions of the teachers dependent to a considerable extent on the results of the examination.

> There can be no doubt that if one teacher finds that his income depends on the condition that his scholars do learn to read, whilst another is paid equally well whether they do so or not, the first will teach more children to read than the second.
>
> *Ibid*, 157.

It was this principle of payment by results, rather than any other recommendation of the Commission, which was adopted. Robert Lowe, the new Vice-President of the Council, issued a revised code of grants in 1862. This simplified the task of paying grants and promised more efficient education. Teachers' salaries became dependent on their pupils' attendance and their ability to pass examinations conducted by the inspectors. The decision to use examinations in the elementary schools reflected the growing interest in examinations and their increasing role in society.

The Revised Code increased attendance at school, and teachers were forced to concentrate on the younger and weaker pupils as well as the brighter children. The dominance of the annual examination led to rote learning and cramming. Schools in poor areas with untrained teachers had the hardest task since they often only managed to qualify for the lowest grant. Relationships between the teachers, the inspectors and the Education Department deteriorated rapidly, and Lowe and Ralph Lingen, the Secretary of the Committee of the Council, faced much criticism. It was said of Lingen:

> He has sat for so long on his stool in Downing Street that I very much question if he has for very many years been inside any of those Schools for which he is legislating in so crude a fashion; and with infatuated blindness he obstinately declines to accept the information which the more experienced and able Inspectors are longing to impart to him. If he had known more of the country, and less of the Department, he would have understood better how to have obtained increased efficiency at much less cost than he has done.
>
> *Education Miscellanies* vol 10, Archives of the Dept of Education and Science.

For the government there was a considerable financial saving. The education grant, which stood at £840,000 in 1862, had fallen to £705,000 two years later. Payments were no longer made directly to the teachers by the state. The school managers received the grant and then paid the teachers. The Revised Code deprived the teacher of additional payments for supervising pupil-teachers. Many took less interest in the pupil-teachers, and there was a decline in the numbers coming forward to train as teachers. In many schools the size of classes increased. From 1867 to 1890 the elementary schools were controlled by the Revised Code. This was gradually modified to admit other subjects and so widen the curriculum.

While strong opinions raged about the advantages and disadvantages of the Revised Code, secondary education was also undergoing examination. Following a Royal Commission on the older universities, attention was drawn to the public schools, and a Royal Commission was appointed (the Clarendon Commission 1861–4). This was followed by an investigation of the endowed schools (the Taunton Commission 1864–7). These schools had enjoyed immunity from state supervision apart from that of the Board of Charity Commissioners, who had been authorised by the Charitable Trusts Act of 1853 to examine the administration of endowments. From 1860 the Commissioners were empowered to reorganise individual charities, and many of those undertaken were educational ones. Apart from this supervision of their endowments, such schools enjoyed great freedom, and change within them was difficult to achieve. Critics of the great public schools particularly wished to see a broadening of the curriculum. Nine schools were chosen for the Clarendon inquiry—two day schools—St Paul's and Merchant Taylors'—and seven public schools which were boarding schools including Eton, Rugby and Shrewsbury. The Commissioners found the curriculum narrow, but approved the teaching of classics for abler boys. However, far too many average boys left school with little knowledge of the classics and no compensating knowledge of modern studies. The Commissioners praised the discipline of moral and religious training given to the boys.

The Commissioners found evidence of change at some of the schools. At Shrewsbury, the Headmaster, Dr Kennedy, had organised a Non-Collegiate Class in response to local feeling. He said:

> An attempt I have made of late years to satisfy that sort of call which exists, and not unnaturally exists, among the community, for an education which shall meet the wants of those classes who do not intend to send their sons to the universities. I call it a 'non-collegiate' class, because I have never allowed the word 'commercial' to enter in among us.
>
> *Report*, vol IV, Shrewsbury Evidence, QQ, 213.

About twelve boys out of 141 in 1861 were studying Latin, French, English composition, modern History and mathematics—the modern subjects replacing Greek and verse-making.

The importance of these great schools as 'the schools of the governing class' is apparent from the Report. They were attended by some 3,000 pupils, who eventually held high positions in the Church, the government, the army and the law. Between 1801 and 1924 a quarter of the Cabinet were Old Etonians:

It is not easy to estimate the degree in which the English people are indebted to these schools for the qualities on which they pique themselves most—for their capacity to govern others and control themselves, their aptitude for combining freedom with order, their public spirit, their vigour and manliness of character, their strong but not slavish respect for public opinion, their love of healthy sports and exercise. These schools have been the chief nurseries of our statesmen; in them, and in schools modelled after them, men of all the various classes that make up English society, destined for every profession and career, have been brought up on a footing of social equality, and have contracted the most enduring friendships, and some of the ruling habits, of their lives; and they have had perhaps the largest share in moulding the character of an English gentleman.

First Part, General Report, 56.

Apart from recommending a widening of the curriculum so that boys from these schools could compete in the civil service examinations and take army and university entrance, the Commissioners were concerned with the management and government of the schools. The Public Schools Act of 1868 confined itself to the administration of the schools. They were required to submit or accept schemes for new governing bodies. The powers of the headmaster were defined, and some out-of-date statutes were modified. The government refused to interfere further in the schools, but in the following years many of the suggestions of the Commissioners, particularly in widening the curriculum, were adopted. Organized games became an increasingly important feature of public school games. The cult of athleticism and the spirit of fair play took the place of much of the bullying and drinking of former public school life. There was considerable praise for the beneficial effects of school sport, and the influence of the schools was felt in the leisure pursuits of society with the development of rugby and football. Considerable claims were made for the value of sport:

An assistant master, who has taken an active interest in what may be termed the physical education of Eton, bears testimony to the beneficial effects, not only physical but moral, of a keen participation in athletic sports. It diminishes, in his opinion, the class of idlers and loiterers—a class by common consent most mischievous to whom too many temptations are offered by the street and little shops of Eton—and is an antidote to luxurious and extravagant habits, to drinking and vice of all kinds.

G. Staunton, *The Great Schools of England* (1865) 36.

The investigation of schools not included in either the Clarendon or the Newcastle Commissions was undertaken by the Schools Inquiry Commission under Lord Taunton. It examined some 782 endowed schools and 122 proprietary and some private schools. Secondary education for girls, as well as for boys, was considered, and evidence from America and Europe as well as Britain was taken. Secondary education was needed for over 904,000 pupils of the middle classes in the 1860s. The Commissioners reflected social views of the time in their attitude to the wishes of parents for educational provision:

> The wishes of the parents can best be defined in the first instance by the length of time during which they are willing to keep their children under instruction. It is found, that viewed in this way, education, as distinct from direct preparation for employment, can at present be classified as that which is to stop at about 14, that which is to stop at about 16, and that which is to continue till 18 or 19; and for convenience we shall call these the Third, the Second, and the First Grade of Education respectively. The difference in the time assigned makes some difference in the very nature of the education itself; if a boy cannot remain at school beyond the age of 14 it is useless to begin teaching him such subjects as require a longer time for their proper study; if he can continue till 18 or 19, it may be expedient to postpone some studies that would otherwise be commenced early. Both the substance and the arrangement of the instruction will thus greatly depend on the length of time that can be devoted to it.

Report of the Royal Commission known as the Schools Inquiry Commission (*Taunton Report*) (1868) I, 15.

The distinctions between the three types of school and the three classes of society expected to attend them was reflected in the curriculum felt appropriate for each age group. Classics dominated the first-grade school; the second grade studied Latin and modern subjects; the third-grade school should provide 'very good reading, very good writing, very good arithmetic' as well as instruction in modern subjects.

The Commissioners found great variations in quality in the schools, particularly among the endowed schools. Some areas had very little secondary provision, and with the exception of schools like Cheltenham Ladies' College and the North London Collegiate School, they found girls' education in a pitiful state.

A summary of their views on girls' education is included in the Report of the Royal Commission on Secondary Education in 1895 which showed the difficulties faced by its protagonists:

In reading the Blue Books of the 1864–68 Commission with their melancholy account of County after County in which all the girls schools from the highest to the lowest were spending their days, and the minds of their pupils, in handing on to yet another generation the frivolous and mischievous traditions of the last; when even the most enlightened headmistresses wrote their regrets at being obliged to see the children entrusted to their charge waste nine hours a week on music, regardless of whether they had sufficient musical ability to give themselves or their friends the faintest pleasure as the result; when it was seriously doubted whether a girl's brains were able to grapple with the difficulties of vulgar fractions, and when it was generally considered that her physical and moral delicacy was so frail, that both would be injured by a written examination to be looked over by a strange man; in reading all this, and much more to the same effect, one's feeling is one of unmixed and thankful satisfaction.

Report of the Royal Commission on Secondary Education, Vol VI (1895) 257–61, from the Report by Mrs Kitchen, Assistant Commissioner.

The Taunton Commissioners recommended a thorough reorganization of education for the middle classes with an administrative board as a central authority and inspection of schools. They proposed examinations to test the efficiency of teaching and the registration of teachers. To many headmasters the prospect of state intervention in schools was unacceptable. Edward Thring, Headmaster of Uppingham, an endowed school which he transformed into a public school with a considerable reputation, gave a lead to this opposition and invited the headmasters of some of the largest endowed schools to a conference. In 1869 the Headmasters' Conference met for the first time at Uppingham. The older public schools later joined the Conference. The headmasters asserted their independence of the government, and in 1873 they persuaded the universities of Oxford and Cambridge to establish a joint board to examine their pupils.

The outcome of the Taunton Commission was the passing of the Endowed Schools Act in 1869. This appointed three special Endowed Schools' Commissioners to supervise the better application of endowments and to extend their benefit to girls. Through the efforts of the Commissioners some 902 schemes were approved, and many endowed schools were revitalized with a modern curriculum. A few offered scholarships to pupils from elementary schools, and many sent pupils to the universities, particularly those in the provinces. By the end of the nineteenth century some sort of educational ladder from the elementary school to the university had come into existence.

Edward Bunney, 'The School of Deportment', an Elegant Establishment for young ladies. Critics of girls' education condemned the undue emphasis on accomplishments and deportment in many nineteenth century schools.

The three commissions had examined the problems of elementary and secondary education. While secondary education was not regarded as a national responsibility, state intervention in elementary seemed essential. This was an indication of the better relationship between social classes in the 1860s. Robert Lowe, writing in the *Quarterly Review* in 1867 revealed the political reasons for haste:

> Political power is henceforth to reside in the poorest class of householders. We dare not leave it in the hands of men who cannot read and write. The most ordinary principles of self-preservation will soon make education the first and highest of political necessities. Those who have hitherto been lukewarm on this question cannot afford to be lukewarm now. All the power and influences, which until the full development of our new democratic institutions still remain to the upper and middle class, must be turned in this direction. We cannot afford to be ruled by ignorant barbarians. For our own sake, if not for that of the poor, the question must be at once confronted.
>
> *Quarterly Review* (1867).

The voluntaryists organized themselves into the National Education Union to defend their interests against the secularists and radicals of the National Education League. To W. E. Forster, Vice-President of the Education Department, fell the task of framing an act acceptable to the various pressure groups so that educational provision could be extended. His compromise allowed the voluntary societies six months to extend their educational effort, and after that time he provided for the state, through school boards, to 'fill the gaps'. By the Cowper-Temple clause, 'In schools hereafter established by means of rates, no catechism or religious formulary which is distinctive to any particular denomination shall be taught'; parents had the right of withdrawal, and the conscience clause applied to all schools receiving government grants. In his speech to the House of Commons, Forster explained the reasons why the government should extend its work in education, a process which can be seen as part of growing government awareness and concern with social problems:

> Upon this speedy provision of education depends also our national power. Civilized communities throughout the world are massing themselves together, each mass being measured by its force; and if we are to hold our position among men of our own race or among the nations of the world we must make up the smallness of our numbers by increasing the intellectual force of the individual.
>
> *Hansard* 1870 3rd series, 199, 455–6.

8

The demand for technical and scientific education

> We have confessed likewise that . . . this is the only country that has neither supplied . . . scientific or artistic instruction to its industrial population; nor, for men of science and art, a centre of action, and of exchange of the result of their labours . . . Yet this country, as the centre of commerce and industry of the world, would seem to require, more than any other, to have these wants supplied; and the Great Exhibition has, in its results, convinced us that unless they be speedily procured, this country will run serious risk of losing that pre-eminent position which now makes its strength and its boast.
>
> *Second Report of the Commissioners of the Great Exhibition* (1852) quoted in Y. ffrenche, *The Great Exhibition* (1950) 283.

A growing concern about industrial expertise and technical advance contrasted strangely with the national pride and apparent success of the Great Exhibition. Those who voiced their fears touched upon fundamental difficulties which seemed to arise from educational deficiencies as much as from technical stagnation. They saw an urgent need to provide more scientific training in secondary schools and universities, and they deplored the low standards of education and widespread illiteracy in elementary schools which made the provision of technical education to any worthwhile standard almost impossible. Perhaps the greatest obstacle to progress was the lack of appreciation of the need for technical instruction in school. The idea of learning skills on the shop floor through apprenticeship together with the example of the self-made man of industry threw doubt on the value of scientific education in school. Government policy towards scientific education was ambivalent until recent times and did little to give a clear direction to policy. This, indeed, was not surprising as there was little enthusiasm for technical instruction from industrialists, businessmen or the labour movement.

In the country as a whole there was a growing interest in science and its application. Following the study of science in the seventeenth century, rapid industrialization in the eighteenth century produced an interest in its practical application. The foundations of the Society of Arts in 1755 to encourage arts, manufactures and commerce in Great Britain and the promotion of lectures and experiments after 1810 by the Royal Institution both showed a desire for 'the diffision of useful knowledge in general'.

In the first half of the nineteenth century the provision of scientific education was mainly confined to adults through the literary and philosophical institutes and the mechanics' institutes. To find science taught in a school as it was in King's Somborne in Dorset was unusual. The Headmaster of the school, the Revd Richard Dawes, described his approach to science teaching:

> After the school had been opened rather more than two years, I began giving to the teachers and the more advanced of the school children short explanations of a philosophic kind and in a commonsense sort of way of the things passing before their eyes, but of the nature of which they had not the slightest conception, such as some of the peculiar properties of metals, glass and other substances in common use; that the air had weight, and how the pressure of the atmosphere helped them to pump up water; enabled them to amuse themselves with squirts and pop-guns: to suck up water, as they call it, through a straw; why the kettle top jumped up when the water was boiling on the fire; why, when they wanted to know whether it boiled or not, they seized the poker, and placing one end on the lid and the other to their ear, in order to know whether it actually boiled . . . These and other things I find so excessively amusing to them, and at the same time so instructive, that I have scarcely missed a week explaining some principle of this nature and questioning them about what had been done before. In subjects of this kind, and to children, mere verbal explanations, as everyone will perceive, are of no use whatever; but when practically illustrated before their eyes by experiments, they become not only one of the most pleasing sources of instruction, but absolutely one of the most useful.
>
> *Report of the Committee of Council on Education for 1847–8*, vol I, 12–18 (Report of the Revd H. Moseley).

In the public schools science instruction was very limited. A course of talks was sometimes given by invited lecturers but the Clarendon Commission revealed the attitudes that hampered the extension of science teaching in the schools. B. H. Kennedy, the Headmaster of Shrewsbury, said of the sciences, 'The natural laws of chemistry, heat, electricity, etc. are not synthetical enough for elementary instruction. They do not furnish a basis for education.' (Report of the Royal Commission appointed to inquire into Revenues and Management of Certain Colleges and Schools (*The Clarendon Report*) IV, 699–700.) While from Winchester the view was expressed:

> If a man is pursuing a science practically and experimentally so as to be making discoveries and carrying it forward to the greater heights of perfection, then he is indeed exercising the highest faculties a man can have; but boys in school cannot do this. They can only be taught what other people have done. They will only get such knowledge second-hand.
>
> *Ibid*, III, 510–12.

While they vindicated the teaching of classics in the public schools, the Clarendon Commissioners expressed strong recommendations for the extension of science teaching:

> Natural science is practically excluded from the education of the higher classes in England. Education with us is, in this respect, narrower than it was three centuries ago, whilst science has prodigiously extended her empire, explored immense tracts, divided them into provinces, introduced into them order and method, and made them accessible to all. This exclusion is, in our view, a plain defect and a great practical evil. It narrows unduly and injuriously the mental training of the young and the knowledge, interests and pursuits of men in maturer life. Of the large number of men who have little aptitude or taste for literature, there are many who have an aptitude for science, especially for science which deals, not with abstractions, but with external and sensible objects; how many such there are can never be known, as long as the only education given at schools is purely literary; but that such cases are not rare or exceptional can hardly be doubted by any one who has observed boys or men . . .
>
> *Ibid, First Part General Report*, 28–33.

Foreseeing the objections to their proposals, the Commissioners argued the case for flexibility in the curriculum so that time could be found for science lessons. They justified their desire for its inclusion by stressing the educational value of science with its cultivation of 'the faculty of observation, . . . the power of accurate and rapid generalization', seeing in science a training for the mind which 'is perhaps the best corrective for that indolence which is the vice of half-awakened minds, and which shrinks from any exertion that is not, like an effort of memory, merely mechanical'. For the schools one of the great difficulties to be faced when introducing science into the curriculum was the shortage of science teachers, and since the schools sent few science candidates to the universities there was little prospect of the deficiency being remedied from the schools' viewpoint, especially as science graduates could find more lucrative posts in industry and government than in the schools. The universities did little to encourage science teaching in the schools. J. M. Wilson said in 1868:

> If the colleges offered scholarships and exhibitions to acknowledge and encourage the study of science at school, then the teaching of science would at once be naturalized in most of the schools which contribute many men to the universities. Up to the present time Oxford has taken the lead in this; Christchurch, Balliol, Merton, Magdalen and New College all encourage science more or less. And their recognition of it, though very small, has been most useful. But at Cambridge very little is done . . . Hence all the abler boys at school are in fact heavily bribed to study either classics or mathematics, even though their genius is for natural science. And from this want of recognition of science by the colleges generally, and from a belief that it is founded on a well-grounded disapproval of science as a part of early liberal education, and from some distrust of it as a possible disturber of classical tradition, schools naturally hang back from taking the step of incorporating natural science with their course of study.
>
> J. M. Wilson in *Essays on a Liberal Education* (1868) ed F. W. Farrar, 288–9.

Despite these difficulties, many public schools developed scientific studies in response to the recommendations of the Clarendon Commission:

> In 1864 the position of Science in Rugby was completely changed by Dr Temple, in deference to the recommendations of the Royal Commission on the nine public schools, published late in 1863.
>
> They recommended that all boys should, at any rate during part of their school life, learn some branch of Natural Science; and that there should be two principal branches, one consisting of Chemistry and Physics, and the other consisting of Physiology and Natural History. New Science Schools were built, very humble indeed compared with the palace in which chemistry is now housed at Rugby, but sufficient for our needs at that time. Dr Temple was anxious to adopt the recommendations of the Commission in the autumn term of 1864, though the difficulties were great. Two hundred and fifty boys would be beginning Science at once, and my old fifty would be going on with it . . .
>
> We set to work at once with immense enthusiasm under Dr Hooker's advice, and worked through the summer term; and we spent the summer holidays delightfully at Barmouth, with Professor George Henslow as our tutor; and with the aid of a party of ladies made collections, and a large series of diagrams for teaching. The spirit of our teaching was unquestionably derived from the brilliant

> Leçons Élémentaires de Botanique fondés sur l'analyse de 50 Plantes Vulgaires par M. Emm. le Maout. That book is a model of what the teaching of such a science ought to be.
>
> Canon J. M. Wilson, *Board of Education Pamphlet, No. 17* (1909) quoted in P. H. J. H. Gosden, *How They were Taught* (1969) 121.

Often the initiative for developing science depended upon the enthusiasm of an individual teacher. At Dulwich College, F. W. Sanderson developed a strong science side, and when Oundle was anxious to extend its science teaching he was appointed Headmaster. He applied to it his enthusiasm for inquiry and research to the whole curriculum—'Real live education—boys marched up to the frontiers of the unknown—to go into the world as pioneers—Darwins—Listers'. For Sanderson scientific study embraced engineering and gardening as well as the study of chemistry, physics and botany. Oundle illustrates the progress made in Science teaching by the end of the century.

The older universities began to expand their science teaching from the middle of the nineteenth century with the establishment of a Natural Science Tripos at Cambridge in 1848 and the founding of the Honour School of Natural Science at Oxford in 1853. The task was a difficult one. Apart from the lack of facilities for teaching as well as laboratories and specialist libraries, the professors and their staffs were poorly paid. The universities rather than the colleges undertook the expense of building and equipping science laboratories, and this created friction with the humanities which were college-based. A syndicate set up by the Cambridge Senate asserted that its members accepted 'the superiority of the study of mathematics and classics over all others as the basis of general education, but were nevertheless of opinion that much good would result from affording greater encouragement to the pursuit of other branches of science and learning which are daily acquiring more importance and a higher estimation in the world'. (V. H. H. Green, *The Universities* (1969) 235.)

Scientists were likely to be at a disadvantage. The growing interest in scientific education elsewhere, particularly at the German universities, stimulated criticism of English shortcomings. To meet the need for modern facilities, the Science Museum was built at Oxford and the Cavendish Laboratory at Cambridge. In 1884 the Royal Commission on Technical Instruction visited Cambridge and reported:

> The Commissioners were informed that, previous to the year 1871, no practical teaching of science was carried on in the University, with the exception of Chemistry. In that year the late Professor Maxwell was appointed Professor of Physics, and designed the Cavendish Physical laboratory presented to the

> University by the Chancellor, The Duke of Devonshire; and Professor Michael Foster was elected as lecturer on Physiology in Trinity College. From the above year, up to the present time, science teaching in almost every branch has been instituted, of at once the most advanced and the most practical character . . .; and there is no doubt that the authorities of the University generally are at the present time fully alive to the importance of these practical scientific studies, and are determined to push forward and coordinate the still somewhat unsystematic efforts which are being made by the different colleges in this direction. The energy and activity which is thus being displayed at Cambridge is very remarkable.
>
> *Second Report of the Royal Commission on Technical Instruction* (The Samuelson Report) vol I (1884), 420.

From their foundation London and the provincial universities founded science departments and medical schools. Often a university, such as Leeds, was established to meet the needs of local industry and trade. Distinguished research work was developed in small, highly specialized departments. At King's College, London, Charles Wheatstone held the chair of physics while carrying out his experiments in electricity and working on the electric telegraph.

Many of the provincial universities reflected not only their responsibilities to local industry, but also their concern with adult education for the immediate neighbourhood. Several local universities originated from adult university extension classes. At Owens College, Manchester, the science subjects were central to the curriculum, and the College provided day and evening classes:

> The number of students of arts and science in the day classes amounts to about four hundred, that in the medical department to nearly three hundred. In addition to the day instruction, which, of course, forms the chief work of the college, systematic courses of evening lectures and laboratory practice exist, for the benefit of the large number of persons who, being occupied in trade or otherwise during the day, are desirous of continuing their education. The number of evening students amounts to about seven hundred, the subjects taught are the same as in the day classes, all the Professors and assistant lecturers taking part in the tuition, and in many subjects several courses are given . . . These college evening classes serve, in the science subjects at least, as an excellent supplement to the ordinary science teaching under the Department of Science and Art, and to the elementary science instruction given in the board schools, placing a high standard of instruction within the reach of all resident in the district.
>
> *Ibid*, 435.

While the provision for science teaching in secondary schools and universities steadily increased, the comparison of British industrial products with their foreign counterparts at the Paris Exhibition of 1867 showed that the provision of better organized scientific and technical instruction was urgently needed. Herbert Spencer, one of the foremost advocates of a scientific education, had published his theories in *Education, Intellectual, Moral and Physical* in 1861. His views were widely influential. He asked, 'What knowledge is of most worth?', and in his discussion he answered:

> Science. This is the verdict in all courts. For direct self-preservation, or the maintenance of life and health, the all important knowledge is—science. For that indirect self-preservation which we call gaining a livelihood, the knowledge of greatest value is—science. For the due discharge of parental functions, the proper guidance is to be found only in—science. For the purposes of discipline, intellectual, moral, religious, the most efficient study is, once more—science. And yet this study, immensely transcending all others in importance, is that which receives the least attention.
>
> Herbert Spencer, *Education* (1861) ch I.

A Royal Commission, led by the Duke of Devonshire, undertook a detailed survey of scientific education. Thomas Huxley, the eminent scientist, made a strong pleas for science in the elementary school:

> My own feeling is that scientific teaching ought to be made a fundamental part of all primary teaching in the kingdom, and to be made a part of the day's work. Unless I am greatly misinformed, the scientific instruction which is now current in the kingdom was the result, so to speak, of a battle between two official departments. I do not know whether I am rightly or wrongly informed, that it was in the teeth of the Education Department that this scientific instruction was introduced; but if such be the case, the fact accounts, I think, for the nocturnal and somewhat surreptitious position which science at present occupies . . . I think that this is the way we have dealt with science, not only in primary education, but in the larger educational bodies in the country; and my hope is to see science made an integral part of the elementary teaching everywhere in the country, and not to have it merely forced upon one department by another, as seems to have been the case formerly.
>
> *Report of the Royal Commission on Scientific Instruction and the Advance of Science* (*The Devonshire Report*) (1872) vol 1, 23–6.

In considering the science teaching already in progress in schools, Huxley referred to the work of the Science and Art Department at South Kensington. The origin of this department can be traced to 1836 when the government voted £1,500 for the establishment of a normal school of design; and from this was developed in 1852 the Department of Practical Art with the task of bringing order to the schools of design. After the Great Exhibition, the scientist, Lyon Playfair, and a civil servant, Henry Cole, were convinced that there must be 'a deliberate cultivation of science and art' if Britain were to face foreign competition successfully. The Prince Consort lent his support to a scheme which led to the setting up of the Science and Art Department in South Kensington in 1853. Its aim was 'to instruct the industrial classes in the principles of science and art', and it pursued its work under the Board of Trade. Its tasks were mainly educational, and as this might bring it into conflict with the Education Department, lines of division were drawn after 1856—'primary or general education under the Education Department and secondary or industrial education under the Department of Science and Art'. Although the two departments shared the same Vice-President, they each pursued independently separate policies.

The first experiments of the Department in encouraging trade schools met with little success, and it was not until Playfair suggested 'payment for results' that it began to develop its work. In 1856 examinations for drawing were introduced and grants paid to schools which entered successful candidates. The system was extended to science three years later, and the numbers of pupils in schools studying science began to increase. Evening classes were started to take advantage of these grants as well. In 1881–2 Salford School Board held science and art classes:

> The classes have been approved by the Science and Art Department and are held under the conditions laid down in the Science Directory. They are all held in the evening and are attended chiefly by members of the industrial class, pupil teachers and assistant teachers. None of the students are children attending elementary schools. The payments made to the teachers consist of the grants received from the Science and Art Department on the results of the May examinations. The teachers receive no other remuneration.
>
> P.R.O. Ed 16/185 Letter to the Education Department, 18/4/1883.

Grammar schools also took advantage of the grants and increased their numbers of pupils when classes were started. To meet the need for trained teachers of science, the Department ran courses for teachers and eventually established training schools.

In addition to promoting examinations and rewards, Cole and Captain John

Donnelly, a young official who was to become the most important man in the Department, were anxious to further science education in elementary schools for older pupils. The work in evening classes was disappointing, and by furthering 'organized science schools' or 'higher grade schools', which provided tuition during the day, the Department hoped for more systematic science training. As early as 1871 the Department wrote to School Boards:

> It appears to my Lords that the Boards elected under that Act [of 1870], if they are willing to charge themselves with the responsibility and will act for the Science and Art Department, may render highly important services towards the furtherance of science and art instruction by making more complete the local organization provided for in these rules [i.e. rules in the Directory for the conduct of local examinations].
>
> *Eighteenth Report of the Science and Art Department* (1871, 32.

The Liverpool School Board decided that elementary science should replace object lessons in their elementary schools and arranged that the pupil-teachers should attend courses of instruction in the pupil-teacher centres. To solve the difficulties faced by schools which had no science teachers the Board made special arrangements:

> The method of teaching the subjects, which has been found by experience to be capable of producing very beneficial results to the scholars, is to combine ordinary lessons by the teachers of the school, with a system of experimental demonstrations given by means of specially appointed demonstrators. The apparatus required for the demonstrations is kept at a central laboratory, and is transferred from school to school as required, by means of a light hand cart. In this way each demonstrator is able to give from 18 to 20 demonstrations per week . . .
>
> In the intervals between the demonstration, the teachers of the respective classes, who are required to be present at the demonstrations, are expected to go over with the children the subject of the demonstration; and in many instances their lessons are illustrated by simple experiments. And in order to enable the teachers (the large number of whom have unfortunately had no special training for the subject) to perform their portion of the work more satisfactorily, a simple textbook has been specially prepared, containing reading lessons on the subjects of the demonstrations, and exercises to be worked by the scholars.
>
> *Second Report of the Royal Commission on Technical Instruction*, vol V (1884) 201–2, Appendix 33, 'Introduction of the Teaching of Science in the Elementary Schools of Liverpool'.

Active school boards were anxious to undertake work beyond elementary education and provide training further than Standard V. These higher classes which were not in the registers of the Education Department were supported by Science and Education Department grants. Since grants were only available for science and art, the curriculum of these 'higher tops' was illiberal and unbalanced, as shown by the timetable for the Manchester Board Central School:

		Each Week			Each Week
		hrs.			hrs.
1	Scripture	$2\frac{1}{2}$	9	French	3
2	Practical Chemistry	$1\frac{1}{2}$	10	Geography	2
3	Theoretical Chemistry	1	11	Arithmetic	2
4	Magnetism and Electricity	1	12	Physical Geography	2
5	Acoustics, Light etc.	1	13	Mechanics	2
6	Physiology	$1\frac{1}{2}$	14	Drawing	3
7	Mathematics	3	15	Preparation	$2\frac{1}{2}$
8	Grammar and Composition	2			

Report of the Royal Commission on Technical Instruction (1884) vol V, Appendix 33, 'Educational Work in Manchester, Liverpool and Oldham'.

The impetus of the Science and Art Department was felt also in the training colleges which presented candidates in art and science. Some of the mechanics' institutes revived their science instruction to take advantage of the grants, and the new polytechnics, such as the Regent Street Polytechnic (1882), had science and art classes among their wide range of activities.

By the end of the nineteenth century, the work of the Department was being widely criticized, but the Bryce Commission of 1895 recognized the contribution it had made to the development of secondary education. The sort of instruction the Department aided was described by the Secretary as 'distinctly secondary instruction except drawing in elementary schools'. (*Bryce Commission*, V, 98–9.) The view that technical instruction and secondary education were synonymous was reinforced by the Technical Instruction Act of 1889, which defined technical instruction as the principles of science and art applicable to industries but excluded the teaching of industrial practice. The London County Council Technical Board interpreted this as 'empowering them to treat technical education as including the whole field of secondary education minus literature and ancient languages'. The limitations of technical instruction, confined as it was to the principles of science and art, may have advanced the provision of secondary education, but it failed to meet the need for vocational and commercial instruction. There was a demand among skilled craftsmen for such instruction, but there were few grants available for it. Moreover, as the Commission revealed, there was little appreciation of the need—'We believe that many workmen are disposed to attach too little value to the importance of acquiring a knowledge of the principles of science because they do not see their application.' (*Royal Commission on Technical Instruction* (1884) vol I, 523.)

Some solution to the problem came with the Revised Code of 1890, which made possible the teaching of practical subjects in evening classes. Subjects such as building instruction, shorthand and typing, commercial knowledge and laundrywork could now be included in the curriculum. Polytechnics as well as school boards developed these evening classes, and trade classes teaching plumbing, printing and plastering were started. Enrolments in vocational subjects increased, and the Consultative Committee Report of 1909 indicated their popularity:

> Nearly half a million students over 17 years of age entered evening classes in 1906–7 ... The majority of these classes are technical in character. They are attended by those who desire to increase their skill in the work by which they earn their living or (especially in the case of women) in those practical home arts, dexterity in which increases the comfort of life and enables more advantageous use of personal income. The weaker side of these adult evening classes is non-technical. Instruction in history, literature and citizenship has hitherto failed to evoke widespread interest among the masses of the people.
>
> *Consultative Committee Report* (1909) 82–4.

The provision of technical and scientific education, like many new branches of the educational system, grew up haphazardly, and from the time of the Taunton Report of 1868 the need for new local machinery to provide efficient administration had been realized. The Samuelson Report suggested:

> It will be necessary to look, in the main, to local resources for any large addition to the funds required for the further development of technical education in this country ... It is to be desired that in the proposed reorganization of local government, power should be given to important local bodies, like the proposed

county boards and the municipal corporations, to originate and support secondary and technical schools in conformity with the public opinion for the time being of their constituents.

Second Report of the Royal Commission on Technical Instruction (1884) vol I, 515.

In 1888 the Local Government Act set up county and county borough councils to undertake many of the tasks of local government earlier performed by ad hoc bodies. By the Technical Instruction Act of 1889 the new local authorities could assume educational powers and levy a 1d rate to supply aid to technical instruction. Further encouragement for local authorities to undertake the support of technical education came with the Local Taxation (Customs and Excise) Act of 1890 when part of the customs and excise revenue was made available for the support of higher education. The Science and Art Department also extended its grants. In 1891 the Technical Instruction (Amendment) Act permitted technical instruction committees to offer scholarships to students wishing to attend schools and colleges outside their own boundaries as well as to aid such institutions by grants. The county and county boroughs throughout the country, working through their technical instruction committees, could provide overall administration to further technical education. The new authorities faced the problem that in areas where there was little provision for secondary education, 'a good secondary education is not only a necessary supplement to, but the very basis of a sound technical education in all its higher branches'. While most authorities supported the extension of technical education, Surrey alone went as far as founding four county grammar schools.

Even when responsibility for technical education was assumed by the county and county boroughs, the development was haphazard since the Technical Instruction Act was not mandatory. The Bryce Commission condemned the confusion caused by the independent development and policy of a number of agencies administering education. In 1899 the Board of Education took over the work of the county committees, the Science and Art Department and the Education Department, and the conflict in the furtherance of science teaching and technical education was at an end. With the passing of the Education Act of 1902 the expansion of technical education slowed down. Many of the organized Science Schools and Higher Grade Schools became secondary schools, and most of the available money was spent on secondary education. It was felt that technical education could not satisfactorily be developed until a good secondary system had been organized. Most parents were anxious for their children to earn wages early, and there was little sympathy for a longer schooling. If a pupil was to advance beyond elementary education, most parents looked to the grammar schools. The Regulations for Secondary Schools of 1904 distinguished secondary schools from technical institutions and classes.

From 1905 a number of junior technical schools developed. They were linked with the technical colleges for further education, using their equipment and staff as well as buildings. The courses offered were practical and gave a pre-apprenticeship training which in some industries was highly valued. The Board of Education officially recognized the Junior Technical Schools in 1912, and they were eligible for state grants which involved them in state inspection.

The Regulations for Secondary Schools of 1904 ensured that science was taught in secondary schools. In planning the curriculum they should devote $7\frac{1}{2}$ hours a week to science and mathematics 'of which at least three must be to science. The instruction in science must be both theoretical and practical.' This stress on the two aspects of science teaching reflects current discussion about it. Moving away from the question and answer character of some purely theoretical lessons, many were now advocating the adoption of the heuristic method in education by which the pupil should be set to find out things for himself by means of experiment and investigation; and this was increasingly adopted in science teaching, though lack of equipment made the development slower than its advocates would have wished.

This did much to make science teaching seem attractive and interesting to pupils. Science teaching now had made definite progress compared with that in other subjects, and it was also getting better textbooks than other subjects. Matthew Arnold wrote in 1872:

> Good compendiums for the teaching of the natural sciences in schools for the people are coming forth; and the advantage of any branch of study possessing good and compendious text-books it is impossible to overrate. The several natural sciences, too, from their limited and definite character, admit better of being advantageously presented by short text-books than such a wide and indefinite subject-matter—nothing less than the whole history of the human spirit—as that which belongs to letters; and this inherent advantage men of skill and talent, like the authors of the text-books I speak of, are just the people to turn to the best account. So that at the very time when the friends of the natural sciences have the public favour with them in saying to letters: 'Give place, you have had more than your share of attention!' their case is still further improved by their being able to produce their own well-planned text-books for physics, and then to say to the friend of letters: 'And this is what you have to offer! this is what you make such a fuss over! this is what you keep our studies out in the cold for!' And, in truth,

while for those branches of study which belong partly to letters, partly to science—language, geography, history—our schools for the people have no text-books meriting comparison with the new text-books in physics, the schools are in a worse plight still when we come to their means of acquainting their scholars with *letters* strictly so called, with poetry, philosophy eloquence.

Leonard Huxley (ed), *Thoughts on Education from Matthew Arnold* (1912) 206–7.

9 Education for all

> The Legislature in 1870 . . . aimed at supplying a gap, . . . filling up the vacuum which voluntary effort had left empty. It was for that object and that object alone that School Boards were called into existence . . . The Act of 1870 successfully carried out this great if . . . limited object . . .
>
> J. S. Maclure, *Educational Documents* (1965) 150.

These words come from the speech of A. J. Balfour, the Prime Minister, when introducing the Education Bill of 1902 into the House of Commons. In that speech he gave some figures which showed (as well as the great efforts made by supporters of the Church Schools) the extent of the success achieved by the School Boards. There were (he said) 5,700 Board Schools compared with over 14,000 voluntary schools, and about 2,600,000 children were educated in Board Schools and over 3,000,000 in voluntary schools. Since the School Boards had only been established for just over thirty years, this was a considerable triumph for them.

Nevertheless, this development had not been achieved without numerous difficulties. As soon as the new Act was passed in 1870, a survey of the educational needs of the country had to be carried out by a number of inspectors of returns, who did not find their task easy, especially in the countryside:

> It appeared that Returns were answers to questions sent by the Department to every parish in the country; What was the population? What schools had they in the parish? What schools outside the parish did they use? and so on. When we had verified the answers, we were to recommend the recognition of such schools as we found to be efficient and to state what further provision was required, with detailed suggestions . . .
>
> This seemed simple. But the word parish gave us infinite trouble. When we speak of a parish, we think of an ecclesiastical district; and we picture a cluster of houses, a long street and an old church. But parliament meant or defined a *civil* parish; that is, a finite area in which a separate rate can be collected. In most

parts of England the difference is immaterial, but . . . in others the movements of population had produced towns which had far outstripped the old centres after which they were named. There was thus much difficulty. Also in the more rural parts of the country the level of education was too low to allow the parish to have reliable representatives. If a school were ordered it would probably be built and managed by a School Board; and in Anglesey the members of the Board would be five men whose opinion on a pig might be accepted, if the pig belonged to a perfect stranger, but on school matters the pig's opinion would be equally valuable.

Sneyd Kinnersley, *H.M.I.* (1908) 7 ff.

When the survey was completed, there were three ways in which a School Board could be established. The district could ask for one; the managers of voluntary schools might announce that they intended to close them and ask for a School Board to take them over; or the Education Department might consider a district deficient in schools and, if after it had given notice the deficiency was not remedied voluntarily, it might order the setting up of a Board. If none of these three methods was put into operation, a District could not be compelled to set up a Board.

In some large towns, such as London, Manchester, Leeds and Birmingham, where the shortage of schools was chronic, Boards were quickly set up, sometimes even before the results of the survey were announced; but elsewhere there was often a struggle of Nonconformists and Liberals against Churchmen and Conservatives. Generally speaking, it was the Nonconformists who were the most eager to form School Boards. They offered their schools to a Board and agitated for one to be set up in their District. The Churchmen, on the other hand, wished to prevent the formation of School Boards, and in some Districts succeeded in doing this right up until 1902. One of these places was Maidstone in Kent, where the Editor of the *Maidstone and Kentish Journal* supported the Conservative contention that the School Board demanded by the Nonconformists would be an unjustified burden on the rates:

In spite of this undoubted truth, that no more schools are wanted now than those now in existence, and those which will be built out of funds already subscribed, the Liberal Town Councillors call upon the Government to spend something like £10,000 of the ratepayers money . . . The Liberal Councillors do not deny that there is ample accommodation, but they seem to think there ought to be a School Board and a School Rate so that the Nonconformists may not be overshadowed by Churchmen.

Maidstone and Kentish Journal, 7th November 1870.

Once the School Boards were set up, they faced several problems. When the elections were held, the result often perpetuated the political and religious rivalries and animosities among their members and hampered their action. The building of new schools brought about financial and other difficulties, but more immediately troublesome for several Boards were the unsatisfactory schools immediately transferred to them by managers who knew that their condition was hopeless. Great was the despair of the Brighton Board when it was asked to take over a school:

> The children had, it appeared, come from a ragged school in Carlton Hill. Of 200 who thus came only 12 could read and none could write. The school was entirely free, the cost of their management, about £200 a year, being defrayed by subscriptions and donations, but they were in debt to the treasurer. The average attendance was 120 boys and girls (only a few of whom were over 12 years of age), but during the present winter it had been less, some of the children, in consequence of the poverty of their parents, having had to go to the workhouse.
>
> Mary Sturt, *The Education of the People* (1967) 319.

The School Boards, with their local attachments and limited financial resources, were not best-fitted to deal with such problems. The objects set before them in 1870 were limited, and their achievements were inevitably circumscribed. Balfour recognized this also in 1902:

> No ad hoc authority now can cover the whole ground of education ... To the educationalist I think I need make no apologies and offer no excuses ... He has long seen a vast expenditure of public money which has yet left this country behind all its Continental and American rivals in the matter of education. He has seen a large average cost per child in our elementary schools, and yet at the same time many of these schools, half starved, inadequately equipped, imperfectly staffed.
>
> J. S. Maclure, *op cit*, 152.

The successes gained by the School Boards were, indeed, uneven. Generally speaking they made least progress in the rural areas. The main reason for this was that the countryside lacked the economic and social forces such as stimulated educational development in the towns. Among these were the growth of trade and industry which brought demands for minimal educational attainments, better educated and more prosperous parents who were aware of the social value of schooling, educationally minded trade unions, better teachers and democratically elected School Boards. The large towns had the most progressive School Boards, and some idea of their achievements may be gained from these notes made by a Headmaster on changes in his Board School in the unpromising area of East London between 1880 and 1900:

> *The boy of 1900 as compared with the boy of 1880:-* Much more docile; insubordination, then endemic, now almost unknown, and if it occurs very likely to be the fault of the teacher. Cheerful and eager now, then often sullen and morose. Relations with teachers generally friendly, often affectionate—no street-calling after them or stone throwing as there used to be. All this, the result of discipline and control at school, reacts beneficially at home. Truancy almost extinct, and when occurring there is usually something in the blood to explain it. Theft rather common, but perhaps more often detected owing to better supervision.
>
> *Personal cleanliness:-* Greatly improved, verminous cases among boys rare, but among girls almost universal. Out of thirty examined, twenty-eight required attention. As to dirt, it is necessary to distinguish between recent dirt got at play and the ancient kind that gives the strong smell. Swimming is taught and has a good effect. The really dirty, seen when stripped, would not be allowed to bathe, but would be sent home to wash there at first. This now seldom happens. The vermin referred to are lice; bugs are rarely seen; but fleas are common, especially on children coming from homes where there is a baby.
>
> *Obscene language:-* Common both in the street and in the home, but not common in the school where, if disagreeable words are heard, they are checked.
>
> *Obscene conduct:-* Very rare. As to boys and girls, the latter are the aggressors.
>
> K. Dawson and P. Wall, *Education, A Documentary Approach* (1969) 34–5.

Of course such changes were due also to social and economic developments as well as the influence of the schools, but their effect was not inconsiderable, and this again varied from school to school even in Districts where the School Boards were progressive. Even the most energetic and conscientious inspectors were sometimes defeated by bad schools which did very little for the children. That such schools existed right until the last days of the School Boards can be seen from the account by Harold Owen, the brother of Wilfred Owen, the poet, of the school he attended for a short time in Birkenhead in the early years of the century:

> My recollection of the school is rather blurred and vague, probably because it was marked with little incident. The other pupils, coming as they did from some of the poorest homes in Birkenhead, were ragged and dirty, always with running

noses and often with running sores. In this place nothing mattered. The master in charge sat at his desk, scanning a piece of newspaper in a dejected and uninterested manner. I can only suppose that his utter indifference to what we did was so genuine that it made no fun for us to be unruly, so that apart from wandering around the classroom, which we all did freely, I can remember no disorder at all. We were all cold and hungry, and I suspect the general physical condition of the school was so low that energy was easily absorbed by merely sitting and vacantly staring.

Harold Owen, *Journey from Obscurity* (1968) vol 1, 21–2.

In contrast with this, there was much that was achieved by those School Boards which were not content with imparting an elementary education that provided a minimum of knowledge and discipline to the children of the poor. One way in which they did this was to establish what were variously called Higher Grade or Central Schools to which the 'higher tops' (i.e. those from standards VII to IX) of the Board Schools were transferred and given a more advanced education. In the later 1870s a number of School Boards began to establish such schools, among the first of these being the Sheffield School Board, which announced its intention in its Report issued in November 1876:

To furnish (in addition to some accommodation similar to that in other elementary schools) a distinct higher department, to which may be drafted deserving and clever pupils from the other schools of the town ... irrespective of class ... and that in addition to the ordinary subjects set forth in the Fourth Schedule of the New Code of the Education Department, viz. Literature, Mathematics, Latin, French, German, Mechanics, Animal Physiology, Physical Geography, Botany and Domestic Economy (for girls) should be taught. There should also be taught other subjects specially bearing upon the industries of this district, which may be taken under the regulations of the Science and Art Department ... such as Drawing, Chemistry, Geology, Minerology, Principles of Mining, Metallurgy, Machine Construction, Steam, Building Construction, etc. In both senior departments special attention should be given to the training of boys and girls intending to become pupil teachers ... To scholars of special ability passing the competitive examinations ... it is intended that aid should be given of a financial character where necessary. Such an arrangement will ... enable scholars to better fit themselves for most useful positions either connected with the industries of the district or with educational work.

J. H. Bingham, *The Period of the Sheffield School Board* (1949) 174.

Such Higher Grade Schools were assisted by the Department of Science and Art, which was prepared to make grants to schools which taught drawing and science, and a number of these schools gained them. Indeed, some School Boards astutely extended the work of their schools by obtaining government grants (under the system of payment by results instituted in 1862) for all children in the standards and supplementing this by whatever the more advanced children could earn from South Kensington. This way of financing the Higher Grade Schools led to the criticism that they placed too much emphasis on the teaching of science subjects.

As well as wishing to extend the range of their education, the Boards came to realize that they would have to provide social services for the children. One of the first problems brought to their attention was the plight of children who were sent to school without having had enough to eat. This occurred especially in large towns during periods of industrial depression and unemployment. At first a number of voluntary societies provided cheap meals for the children, but soon these were supplemented by the teachers and managers of the schools. Sheffield was a pioneer here also, and in 1893, in reply to an inquiry from the Education Department, the School Board stated:

> In the winter months, and more particularly while the weather was so severe as to stop outdoor work, a considerable amount of distress existed in this district, and a number of children were unable to obtain food before attending school. Assistance has, however, been given in connection with the Society for the Prevention of Cruelty to Children; about 800 per day being supplied with soup and bread. At one school, too, about 80 children are on the average supplied with breakfast daily during the winter months, while other Managers have provided soup at midday for smaller numbers. The teachers at various schools regularly deal with isolated cases of distress, and relief has also been given to a small extent from other sources. As a rule, however, it is believed that very few children in Sheffield are sent to school before obtaining food during the open weather, though there are the usual cases of distress arising through the neglect or bad conduct of the parents. The teachers report that in a number of instances in which children have been sent to school before obtaining breakfast, this arose through the parents not rising sufficiently early.
>
> *Ibid*, 238.

Even more serious was the problem of illness, which was probably the main cause of the absence of children from school. From 1877 the Education Department imposed stringent regulations upon school managers requiring the exclusion of children who were suffering from infectious diseases and the closing and cleansing of buildings during epidemics. These school closures might last for several weeks, while children might be away from school for three or four months because other children in their family or even their street might be suffering from an infectious disease. And yet still the epidemics continued. The unsatisfactory medical situation prevailing in London schools in the 1890s was condemned in 1900 in a striking memorandum by Graham Wallas, Chairman of the Board's School Management Committee and an outstanding scholar and member of the Fabian Society:

> London stands almost alone among the great civilised cities of the world in making no provision for the periodical medical visitation of its schools . . . As long as it was supposed that . . . were mainly communicated by dirt or deficient drainage, or by infected rooms, it was reasonable to rely on the sanitation, closing and disinfection of school buildings . . . [But] the experience of the whole civilised world indicates that the closing of schools and burning of sulphur is an ineffectual . . . method of fighting disease . . . Indeed, if we for a moment put ourselves into the position of those whom we compel to send their children to our Schools, . . . what is it that we should fear for our own children if they went to the Board Schools? Is it not chiefly the possibility of infection, not only with such terrible diseases as Diptheria and Scarlet Fever, but with complaints such as Ringworm and the Ophthalmia which is always to be found in certain districts of London?
>
> David Rubinstein, *School Attendance in London 1870–1904* (1969) 78.

Wallas concluded that medical inspection of the children themselves, and not merely the building in which they were taught, was an essential reform. The London School Board had already, in fact, appointed a school medical officer in 1890, but not until 1903 was he given sufficient assistant medical officers, oculists and nurses to enable school inspections to be carried out, and several other Boards did the same about this time. The South African War of 1899–1902, when many potential recruits were rejected for medical reasons, did much to bring about this development and prepare the way for the setting up of regular school medical services soon afterwards.

Not long after the passing of the Act of 1870 several School Boards realized that they would have to do more than concern themselves with the occasional epidemics and diseases suffered by ordinary children. The Act intended that School Boards should provide elementary education for all children. It made no exception, though it did not contain any specific mention of deaf, blind and other handicapped children. The London School Board was the first to make some provision for them. It opened special classes for them in the later 1870s, and its example was followed by other Boards in large towns. Some of these classes were completely segregated from the sighted and hearing children, but others were in ordinary schools. Some classes were considered by Her Majesty's Inspectors to be grant earning, while other Boards claimed no grants because they feared that what they were doing might be considered illegal by the Education Department. In 1893, however, the Elementary Education (Blind and Deaf Children) Act required the Boards to provide for these children and specified the grant payable. In 1897 the Senior Inspector of such classes reported on the situation in the country:

> The year has been marked by steady progress. This progress is greatest in large centres of population, where philanthropic agencies can most easily reach afflicted children and spread a knowledge of the provisions made for their education, but these provisions are rapidly becoming known even in smaller towns and country districts . . .
>
> Some school authorities have as yet done very little, in some cases perhaps from ignorance of their statutory duties and powers, but in a majority from apathy: a few afflicted children in a widely scattered area are quite easily forgotten by a school attendance committee . . .
>
> My attention has been called, in the course of another inquiry, to the considerable number of feeble-minded blind and deaf children which unhappily exists . . .
>
> *Parliamentary Reports, 1897.*

The Leeds School Board was among the earliest to provide elementary education for such afflicted children, and the same report described the provision made by it for deaf children during the year 1896:

> The elder girls have had regular lessons in dressmaking; a sewing machine has been provided, and useful garments have been made at the class. Instruction in cooking is carried on at the adjoining grade school. The deaf girls form a separate class and receive their cookery instruction in the Friday morning. The lessons are popular with the children, and the presence of one of our own staff to explain the directions has not been necessary.
>
> Physical training receives as much attention as possible. All classes are doing interesting work in hand and eye training . . .

The optical lantern continues to play an important part in our school routine, and a special course of lessons with limelight views has again been successful. During the summer months parties of the children have been taken to the art galleries, and it is intended to pay occasional visits to museums and other places of education and interest.

Ibid.

The overriding problem facing the School Boards, however, was that of attendance. The Boards were established to provide school places where there was a deficiency, but for some years there were, especially in the manufacturing towns, places provided which were not used by the children. The idea of compulsory schooling was entirely new in 1870, though the Act allowed the Boards to make attendance compulsory if they wished. Within a year the Boards in London and twenty-six other places, mostly large towns, were operating their own schemes for compulsory attendence; the number steadily increased, and from 1876 a series of acts made compulsion universal, and in 1891 most elementary school fees were abolished. The need to enforce attendance was intensified under the system of 'payment by results', which lasted from 1862 to 1890, because the amount of government grant which a school earned depended partly upon regular attendance. Nevertheless, enforcement was difficult. Parents wanted their children to be at work, and rural Boards had to face the demands of important farmers for the labour of their pupils on the land. Moreover, public opinion was often against compulsion, and magistrates might give Board attendance officers little help. An incident at the Woolwich Police Court in 1886 illustrated their attitude. When, after the hearing on a case, the London School Board superintendent asked the magistrate, Mr Shiel, to direct that the fee paid for the summons should be repaid to the Board:

Mr Shiel replied that it was his invariable practice not to allow costs or fees to the Board and that he should always adopt this course. The fact was that he wanted the public to know what these prosecutions cost, to which he (the superintendent) replied that any ratepayer could have this information, as, under the Act of Parliament, all the Board's books were open for inspection at any reasonable time. He (the superintendent) further pointed out to Mr Shiel that he was really placing a penalty upon the School Board for carrying out the duties imposed upon it by Act of Parliament; and that it seemed the Board was placed upon a different level to any other informant. The magistrate replied that this was so, the Board *were* on a different level, and as to the question of losing their fees, he did not think there was much in that, as it was merely a question of account, and it did not matter if it came out of one pocket or the other. He (the superintendent) urged upon Mr Shiel that it really did matter so far as the Board were concerned, and that he could be no party to any understanding. He felt bound to make a special application in each case, inasmuch as, according to his reading of the section, it was clearly contemplated that the court was to exercise a discretion in the matter. He could not see what discretion was used when the magistrate made it a rule to allow no costs in this or in future cases. The application was, however, refused, but he renewed it in every other case before the court, to which Mr Shiel simply replied 'No'.

Second Report of the Royal Commission on the Elementary Education Acts (1887) extracts from the Minutes of the London School Board.

One of the main reasons why it was difficult for the School Boards to compel working-class children to attend school was the poverty of their homes. Wretched housing conditions produced an environment hostile to formal education; the destitution of parents led them to want their children to go out to work as soon as possible; and for poor people, education was not relevant to their daily toil upon which their lives depended. In 1883 T. Marchant Williams, a London School Board inspector, laid stress on bad housing conditions, instancing three schools in the Finsbury division in which 58, 82 and 85 per cent of the contributing families lived in one room:

How is it possible, I ask, for the best Teachers to cope with the overwhelming difficulties which are implied by such facts as these, which, by the way, are typical of a large number of Schools of the London School Board. The Teachers of the Tower Street School work with all the energy and ability they can command, and they are materially aided by a careful and judicious Visitor; but they cannot house or feed the little children, nor can they clothe them; all they can seem to be able to do is to attract a handful of them to School in time to learn (but not to understand) a few texts and a few facts from the Bible, and about 70 per cent of them (on an average) to learn imperfectly the subjects prescribed for them in the Code. To any of the half-starved children of Seven Dials, St Luke's, Lisson Grove and Saffron Hill, the forty days' fasting in the wilderness and the miraculous feeding of 'five thousand men, besides women and children', with five loaves and two fishes, appear too commonplace, I should say, to excite much comment. It is really most difficult for the Inspectors to know what results to expect from a year's teaching of these ill-housed, ill-clad and ill-fed little children.

Quoted, D. Rubinstein, *op cit*, 58.

As public concern for education grew, there was a greater awareness of these and other problems facing the School Boards. Among such problems, the one that probably gained most popular prominence was that caused by the relationship of the Board Schools and the voluntary schools. Although many of the older Nonconformist leaders had been opposed to state education, the Nonconformists as a whole had relinquished their efforts to support their schools after 1870. British and Methodist Schools had steadily been handed over to the local School Boards. The Church of England, on the other hand, had been determined to maintain its schools, and as the result of heroic money-raising efforts by the clergy had succeeded in increasing after 1870 the number of Church Schools and the proportion of the country's children educated in them. The Roman Catholics had also added to the number of their schools, especially in the large industrial towns and ports where Irish immigrants settled.

The voluntary schools, however, steadily ran into financial difficulties. Their income was never sufficient. Money raised by voluntary subscriptions, collections and bazaars could never rival the sums the Board Schools could draw from their compulsory rates. Complaints about the position of the voluntary schools as the result of the Act of 1870 by the Roman Catholics led by Cardinal Manning and supported by the leaders of the Church of England brought about the appointment of the Royal Commission on the Elementary Education Acts, which produced its report, the Cross Report, in 1888. It recommended changes in the organization of elementary education which were to be carried out in 1902:

> We think that if, in the impending reorganization of the local government of the country, education were recognized as one of most important branches of that local government, and arrangements were made for gradually connecting it, more or less, with the civil administration of each locality, much of the unhealthy competition between the two school systems would disappear, and the expenditure caused by their rivalry would be reduced. Such an arrangement would also tend to decentralize the present system in a way of natural local development, relieving the Education Department of innumerable administrative details, and largely reducing the cost of its staff, while retaining for the Education Department powers of general control which have been of the greatest value to education in the past . . . We think it reasonable and just that the supporters of voluntary schools should retain the management of these schools on condition of bearing some substantial share of the burden of the cost in subscriptions. But it does not seem either just or expedient to allow the voluntary system to be

gradually destroyed by the competition of board schools possessing unlimited resources at their command. We therefore recommend that the local education authority be empowered to supplement from local rates the voluntary subscriptions given to the support of every public State-aided elementary school in their district to an amount equal to these subscriptions, provided it does not exceed the amount of ten shillings for each child in average attendance.

The Cross Report (1888), Final Report, Part V, ch 3, 194.

10 New foundations

> There is one feature of this growing concern of the State with education which must not here be overlooked. The growth has not been either continuous or coherent; i.e. it does not represent a series of logical or even connected sequences. Each one of the agencies whose origin has been described was called into being, not merely independently of the others, but with little or no regard to their existence. Each has remained in its working isolated and unconnected with the rest. The problems which Secondary Education present have been approached from different sides, at different times, and with different views and aims. The Charity Commissioners have had little to do with the Education Department and still less with the Science and Art Department. Even the borough councils have, to a large extent, acted independently of the school boards, and have, in some instances, made their technical instruction grants with too little regard to the parallel grants which were being made by the Science and Art Department. Endowments which, because applied to elementary education, were exempted from the operation of the Endowed Schools Acts, have still been left exempt; though the public provision of elementary education in 1870 and the grant of universal free elementary education in 1891 have wholly altered their position. The University Colleges, though their growth is one of the most striking and hopeful features of the last thirty years, remain without any regular organic relation either to elementary or to Secondary Education, either to school boards or to county councils. This isolation and this independence, if they may seem to witness to the rich variety of our educational life, and to the active spirit which pervades it, will nevertheless prepare the observer to expect the usual results of dispersed and unconnected forces, needless competition between the different agencies and a frequency overlapping of effort, with much consequent waste of money, of time and of labour.
>
> *The Bryce Report* (1895) quoted in J. S. Maclure, *op cit*, 142–3.

The Bryce Commission was appointed to consider the best methods of establishing a well-organized national system of secondary education. Its appointment reflected a growing concern about the haphazard growth of 'secondary' schools and an interest by radicals like the Fabians in the extension of educational opportunity. It was clear that interdepartmental jealousies in the central educational administration hindered progress. It was said that 'the secondary schools are administered by gentlemen for gentlemen, the elementary schools by men for men, but the technical schools by cads for cads'. (Anonymous quotation in G. A. N. Lowndes, *The Silent Social Revolution* (1937) 61.)

A necessary preliminary to educational progress was the Board of Education Act of 1899. This established under the direction of a President a Board of Education to which were transferred the powers of the three departments—the Education Department, the Charity Commission and the Science and Art Department. The Board was advised by a Consultative Committee which in due course prepared many important reports on educational subjects.

One of the problems in co-ordinating a system of national education was the existence of over 2,500 School Boards with whom the Board had to deal individually. The problem was further complicated when an auditor of the Local Government Board, named Cockerton, declared that part of the expenditure of the London School Board concerned purposes other than elementary education. In the legal battle that followed the judge drew attention to the interpretation of the term 'elementary'. He felt that education given to pupils of sixteen or seventeen years was in reality secondary education. Robert Morant, a leading civil servant at the Board of Education, saw this case as an opportunity to redefine and reorganize elemetary and secondary education. With the findings of the Cross and Bryce Commissions as well as foreign examples as a guide, he prepared a new education act for A. J. Balfour, the Prime Minister:

> Within a few days the Education Bill will be placed on the Statute Book, and a new educational era will have opened with the passing into law of a measure destined to be more important in its consequences than the famous Compromise and Act of 1870. The Act of 1902 is not a compromise. It represents a national educational policy maintained and developed during a parliamentary struggle extending over a period of nearly nine months, a policy that may hereafter be modified to meet a rising standard of educational efficiency, but one which can never be reversed. The Bill has committed the nation beyond recall to the principles that the State has duties to perform with respect to every aspect of education, that the 'general co-ordination of all forms of education' is a national affair, and that denominationalism in schools is at least as consistent with state aid as undenominationalism. Nine months of battle in the country, fifty-five

> sittings in the House of Commons, floods of impassioned oratory, torrents of vehement invective, dark and mysterious threats of vengeance to come, have all left essential features of the Bill unaltered.
>
> *The Spectator*, 13th December (1902) 'Topics of the Day'.

Morant achieved the passing of an act which brought to an end the School Boards and gave responsibility for organizing both elementary and secondary education to the local authorities. It ensured that children attending voluntary schools would receive equal facilities with those attending undenominational schools as both were given rate-aid. The local educational authorities were empowered to provide education other than elementary: 'For the first time the Bill definitely includes as a public function, education as education, not primary education only or technical education only, but anything and everything that is education from the kindergarten to the university. This renders the Bill of 1902 epoch-making in the history of English education.' (Article by S. Webb, *Daily Mail*, 17 October 1902.)

Bitter controversy followed the passing of the Act, not aroused, as might have been expected by the abolition of the school boards, but by the rate-aid given to voluntary schools. The Liberals and the Nonconformists, led by David Lloyd George and Dr Clifford, a baptist minister, organized passive resistance to the Act by non-payment of rates, while some local education authorities neglected their duties to voluntary schools. Parliamentary action eventually ended the opposition. The Liberals and Nonconformists made a further attempt to end the favoured position of the voluntary schools when the Liberal party was returned to power in 1906. Three bills were introduced and were later withdrawn. After their failure, the plans of 1902 served as a basis for the local administration of education until the modifications of the 1944 Act.

Morant undertook the task of restructuring England's educational system by clearly defining the ways he wished changes to take place. In the spring of 1903 he produced the first of a series of 'Regulations' to guide teachers and local authorities. These expressed the guiding principles he saw in his task. The first, 'Regulations and Instructions for the Training of Pupil Teachers', stressed the need for a well-trained teaching force. In the Elementary Code of 1904 new ways of computing the grant were introduced and did much to liberalize the elementary schools. The introduction to the Code stated the aims for elementary schools:

> The purpose of the Public Elementary School is to form and strengthen the character and to develop the intelligence of the children entrusted to it, and to make the best use of the school years available, in assisting both girls and boys, according to their different needs, to fit themselves, practically as well as intellec-

tually, for the work of life . . .

And, though their opportunities are but brief, the teachers can yet do much to lay the foundations of conduct. They can endeavour, by example and influence, aided by the sense of discipline, which should pervade the School, to implant in the children habits of industry, self-control, and courageous perseverance in the face of difficulties; they can teach them to reverence what is noble, to be ready for self-sacrifice, and to strive their utmost after purity and truth; they can foster a strong respect for duty, and that consideration and respect for others which must be the foundation of unselfishness and the true basis of all good manners.

The Elementary School Code (1904).

The Times was one of many journals which welcomed the statement as a departure from the barren instructions meted out to elementary schools in the previous decades. To Morant the building of an efficient secondary system was 'perhaps the most vital portion of educational provision'. When the growth in secondary education became apparent, he wrote to a friend, 'If you can really feel what you say as to the Day Secondary Schools having at last been established, there is nothing in the world I could have better wished as an epitaph, for that was my fundamental wish in 1902.'

The secondary provision consisted of the endowed grammar schools, which could be supported by local authority grants after 1902, and the municipal or county secondary schools set up and maintained by the councils. Often a higher grade school, organized science school or pupil teacher centre changed its character to become a secondary school after 1902. In 1904 the Board of Education issued its regulations for secondary schools which determined the nature of secondary education and was designed to produce a balanced curriculum unlike the imbalance of a vocational secondary education which had existed in the Higher Grade Schools and Morant feared might be introduced by the local authorities into the new municipal schools:

For the purposes of these Regulations, therefore, the term 'Secondary School' will be held to include any Day or Boarding School which offers to each of its scholars, up to and beyond the age of 16, a general education, physical, mental and moral, given through a complete graded course of instruction of wider scope and more advanced degree than that in Elementary Schools. The Board desire to emphasize the three following points as being essential to this course of instruction:

(*a*) The instruction must be general; *i.e.*, must be such as gives a reasonable degree of exercise and development to the whole of the faculties, and does not confine this development to a particular channel, whether that of pure and applied Science, of literary and linguistic study, or of that kind of acquirement which is directed simply at fitting a boy or girl to enter business in a subordinate capacity with some previous knowledge of what he or she will be set to do . . .

(*b*) The course of instruction must be complete; *i.e.* must be so planned as to lead up to a definite standard of acquirement in the various branches of instruction indicated above, and not stop short at a merely superficial introduction to any one of them.

Regulations for Secondary Schools (1904).

The curriculum prescribed for the secondary schools was strongly based on the tradition of the grammar and public schools with an academic bias. In 1907 Supplementary Regulations for Secondary Schools created a scholarship system to link elementary and secondary education for the ablest pupils:

In all Schools where a fee is charged, arrangements must be made to the satisfaction of the Board for securing that a proportion of School places shall be open without payment of fee to scholars from Public Elementary Schools who apply for admission, subject to the applicants passing an entrance test of attainments and proficiency such as can be approved by the Board . . .

The proportion of School places thus required will ordinarily be 25 per cent of the scholars admitted.

Supplementary Regulations for Secondary Schools (1907) ch 3, 5.

Scholarship examination became very competitive as demand for secondary education grew, and there was considerable discussion about methods of testing pupils at a time when there was a growing interest in psychology. These examinations had a considerable influence on the curriculum and organization of the elementary schools where much extra time was often devoted to the scholarship class. Academic standards in the new secondary schools were nurtured by the formation of bodies like the Historical Association in 1906 and the Geographical Association in 1893 to foster knowledge and interest in particular subjects. Examinations proliferated as secondary education expanded so that the variety of demands being made on the pupils led to concern, and in 1911 the Consultative Committee examined the effects of examinations. They concluded that external examinations were desirable, but that their number and type should be regulated. In the same year Miss Florence Gadesden, Headmistress of Blackheath High School, expressed her views on the use and abuse of examinations:

University and other examinations have done excellent work and obviously cannot be altogether abolished. But now that the standard of school work is sufficiently high, and that the teachers know thoroughly what is good while also knowing the capacities of their pupils, it is time the schemes of examinations should be remodelled. The academic qualifications of the teachers are as good as those of the examiners—their other qualifications for their work are often better—but they are too often discouraged by the rigid requirements of examining bodies and by want of appreciation of all originality. While, therefore, recognizing their value and even necessity, I plead for greater elasticity in examinations and that a larger voice in judging results be given to the teacher.

Sara A. Burstall and M. A. Douglas (eds), *Public Schools for Girls* (1911), 253.

In the elementary schools teachers began to enjoy greater freedom in their work. The *Handbook of Suggestions for the Consideration of Teachers*, issued by the Board in 1905, not only in its title indicated the new approach, but stressed that:

The only uniformity of practice that the Board of Education desires to see in the teaching of Public Elementary Schools is that each teacher shall think for himself, and work out for himself such methods of teaching as may use his powers to the best advantage and be best suited to the particular needs and conditions of the school.

Handbook of Suggestions for the Consideration of Teachers and Others Concerned in the Work of Public Elementary Schools (1905) 6.

However, H. C. Dent recalled from his own experience that a pupil in an elementary school at this time was unlikely to be aware of a changing attitude:

I was a pre-adolescent pupil in an elementary school in 1904. Like millions more, I intoned my way monotonously (and uncomprehendingly) through the multiplication tables; I was bored to nausea by the one and only 'Reader' we were allowed each year—which had to serve the dual function of giving us practice in the mechanics of reading aloud (why aloud?) and of being our introduction to English life and letters. I wrote, endlessly, in 'copy-books' morally elevating maxims—'A stitch in time saves nine', 'Too many cooks spoil the broth'—but I never composed, much less wrote, in class a single original sentence. I memorized, in rhyme, the names and idiosyncrasies of the English kings and queens

William the Conqueror long did reign,
William his son by an arrow was slain . . .

and I memorized (though not in rhyme) the names of the capes, bays, county towns, mountains and rivers, literally all round Britain. And once each week I painted blobs (we called them flowers), and wove wet reeds into work baskets: the school's sole concessions to 'activity'.

Not much in all that to 'form and strengthen the character', or 'develop the intelligence', or 'make the best use of the school years', or fit children, either 'practically' or 'intellectually', 'for the work of life'. And this experience of mine, I must emphasize, was not in the class of a cynical, dull or apathetic teacher, but of a lively, intelligent, warm-hearted woman, who as a person did us boys and girls a world of good. Did she know no other way to teach? Or was she bound by the school timetable?—that sacroscant nineteenth-century visual aid, put up 'in a prominent position' (as the Code required) by the new head teacher when he arrived, and never taken down until he left, it might well be thirty years later. (Men did not move then as they do now. Nor did women, for that matter; the age of the 'dedicated spinster' was just beginning, as one LEA after another refused to employ married women.)

Such teaching as I endured went on for many years in many schools after 1904.

H. C. Dent, *1870–1970 A Century of Growth in English Education* (1970) 69.

Some teachers were interested in new methods and new ideas like those of John Dewey. Project work, which encouraged the child to learn by activity, and creative handwork found a place in the schools. For young children there was an increasing emphasis on the methods of Froebel and Madame Montessori which encouraged self-expression. Some schools, particularly the new progressive schools like Bedales, adopted the Dalton plan:

What it implies is letting the child use the classroom as he uses (or should be allowed to use) a laboratory, to obtain knowledge at first hand, under the guidance of the teacher, but by his own active research, instead of waiting passively with the other members of the class to have it put before them in fixed quantities only and at fixed times.

J. H. Bradley, *An Educational Experiment at Bedales School.*

A changing attitude to the child influenced the relationships between pupil and teacher in school. Homer Lane, an American who established a self-governing community for young people, 'The Commonwealth', typified this new outlook:

> Lane's conscious reason for believing in his 'self-government' can be found in one of his early Reports. 'It is not necessary', he wrote in 1915, 'to emphasize the now generally accepted principles of new education . . . that when adult domination of the child is supplanted by adult respect for the child and encouragement of his activities, the self-expression of the adolescent will be beneficient. The individual child will always experiment to a great or lesser extent in wrong-doing, thereby discovering for himself ethical truths, far more potent in developing self-restraint than ethical opinions imposed by autocratic authority.
>
> J. H. Simpson, *Schoolmaster's Harvest* (1954) 145.

Prompted by the work of pioneers like Rachel and Margaret McMillan, who opened their first school clinic at Bow, in 1904 there was a growing concern for the welfare of children, and this led to a widening conception of the State's responsibility. Educationalists had been aware of the needs of the child from the poor home since the days of the school boards, and a committee of inquiry into physical deterioration made the problem more widely known. Morant was keenly interested in the physical welfare of children, and legislation was passed which made it possible for local educational authorities to provide school meals and compel them to undertake the medical inspection of children in elementary schools. In the schools subjects like hygiene, physical education and domestic science were developed. Morant established a medical department at the Board of Education under Dr George Newman. He developed the School Medical Service which contributed greatly to the improvement of the health of schoolchildren.

The McMillans drew attention to the needs of the pre-school child. Rachel said, 'We must begin further back with the children and their mothers before the little ones come to school. Five years is too late.' In 1911 they opened a nursery school at Deptford. The First World War interrupted their work, but eventually provision was made for nursery school education in the Education Act of 1918.

If little was done for the pre-school child, some provision was made for the older pupil who did not transfer from the elementary to the secondary school. After Morant's fall from office in 1911, some local education authorities opened Central Schools and Junior Technical Schools. These provided for pupils who wanted to stay beyond the minimum leaving age of twelve and gave them some form of post-elementary education often with a vocational bias.

With the outbreak of war in 1914, educational progress was seriously hindered, but a measure of the changes that had taken place for the child at school are well described in an inspector's report of the period:

Drill at the Hugh Myddleton School, London 1907

The child's life in school is being brought into closer relation with his life out of school; the barrier which tradition has erected between the two is being broken down. Education is less bookish and more practical than it was. In almost every subject in the curriculum, in English and Arithmetic, hardly less than in Nature Study and Geography, the teacher of to-day uses the materials and experiences with which the children are familiar in everyday life . . . At the same time, the influence of the school is spreading more and more widely over the whole sphere of the child's interests and activities. The school concerns itself with his bodily as well as with his mental and moral development, with his amusements as well as with his labours, or teaches him to use his hands as well as his head, to play as well as to work.

Board of Education Reports (1910–11 to 1915–16) 40.

Books for further reading

Of the many general histories of English education during this period, three might be mentioned: J. W. Adamson, *English Education 1789–1902* (CUP, 1964), H. C. Barnard, *A Short History of English Education 1760–1944* (University of London Press, 1947), and B. Simon, *Studies in the History of Education 1780–1870* (Lawrence & Wishart, 1960).

Books on elementary education are G. A. N. Lowndes, *The Silent Social Revolution 1895–1965* (OUP, 1969), M. Sturt, *The Education of the People* (Routledge, 1967), and J. S. Maclure, *One Hundred Years of London Education* (Allen Lane 1970). Secondary Education is covered by R. L. Archer, *Secondary Education in the Nineteenth Century* (Cass, 1966), and O. Banks, *Parity and Prestige in English Secondary Education* (Routledge, 1955).

Developments in the public schools are described in T. W. Bamford, *Thomas Arnold* (Cresset, 1960), and T. W. Bamford, *The Rise of the Public Schools* (Nelson, 1967); and in the progressive schools in W. A. C. Stewart and W. P. McCann, *The Educational Innovators 1750–1967* (Macmillan, 2 vols, 1967–8). On the universities there is V. H. H. Green, *The Universities* (Pelican, 1968), and on technical education M. Argles, *South Kensington to Robbins* (Longmans, 1964). A simple book on the teaching profession is M. Ballard, *The Story of Teaching* (Longmans Young Books, 1969).

The story of the education of women is told in J. Kamm, *Hope Deferred* (Methuen, 1965).

Finally, a very interesting selection of illustrations is to be found in M. Seaborne, *Education* (Studio Vista, 1966).

Books for further reading

[illegible]

[illegible]

[illegible]

[illegible]

Index